praise for Paula Huston's *books*

"An amazing, lovely, important book. Artful, wise."
—RON HANSEN
author of *Mariette in Ecstasy* and *Exiles*

"Paula is already one of those seasoned souls one comes
to depend on, both for her well of refreshing knowledge,
and for the wisdom that comes with such knowledge."
—PAUL MARIANI
author of *Deaths & Transfigurations*

"Paula has fully lived what she writes."
—LUCI SHAW
author of *Water My Soul* and *What the Light Was Like*

"Paula Huston has much in common with Kathleen
Norris and Henri Nouwen . . . [She is] a credible
witness to what happens when God is chosen as the
center of one's life."
—*America: The National Catholic Weekly*

"With honesty and an open-armed embrace of her
own fallibility, Huston pulls readers in, showing how
odd and downright contrary it can feel to engage in a
monastic discipline—and yet how fulfilling."
—*Los Angeles Times*

forgiveness

following Jesus into radical loving

PAULA HUSTON

PARACLETE PRESS
BREWSTER, MASSACHUSETTS

Forgiveness: Following Jesus into Radical Loving

2008 First Printing

Copyright © 2008 by Paula Huston

ISBN: 978-1-55725-570-9

Library of Congress Cataloging-in-Publication Data

Huston, Paula.
  Forgiveness : following Jesus into radical loving / by Paula Huston.
    p. cm.
  Includes bibliographical references.
  ISBN 978-1-55725-570-9
  1. Forgiveness—Religious aspects—Christianity. 2. Forgiveness of sin. I. Title.
  BV4647.F55H87 2008
  234'.5--dc22
                                        2008033820

10 9 8 7 6 5 4 3 2 1

Published by Paraclete Press
Brewster, Massachusetts
www.paracletepress.com
Printed in the United States of America

contents

introduction

FOR MANY YEARS, my younger brother, now one of my favorite people, was my nemesis. No matter how our battles started—and they were physical and fierce—when it came time for the parental judgment call, I was invariably found to be at fault. This, I thought, was grossly unfair. No matter that I was four years older. From my perspective, he was the privileged male child, exempt from scullery duty and paid—paid!—to mow the lawn, a job I passionately, irrationally, coveted. Plus, he was a tease, a conniving little beast who knew every weak and rotted plank in my character and purposely slammed his high-top Keds (I was jealous of them, too) down hard whenever he saw the opportunity. I blamed him for my having to serve time in the corner while the happy shrieks of the neighborhood kids drifted through the window like the life that was passing me by. I was convinced (completely wrongly, of course) that my mother loved him more than she loved me, and this precipitated clumsy, frantic efforts on my part to gain her attention. But no matter how I slaved for As at school or tried to impress her with my writing skills, I could not seem to pry his grubby little fingers off her heart.

However, one rainy afternoon all this changed. We kids were restless and bored and the situation was degenerating rapidly. I could see that look in his eye; he was plotting, I was sure of it, and soon full-blown teasing would erupt. And then I would hit him, and I would be in the corner again, and he would spend the rest of his day darting smirkily past me in my invisible cell. But somehow, our sister saved us; she plopped a record on the turntable and started to hum and spin. Though neither my brother nor I can put a finger on what happened next—no words were exchanged, or at least none that we can remember—we suddenly found ourselves locked in one another's arms, slow dancing to "String of

Pearls." I was twelve, he was eight, and not since he was a baby in his basinet (my baby, I'd thought of him then) had I adored him so honestly and purely: so protectively.

In a twinkling, we'd been released from mutual hostility, from blaming and recrimination, from smoldering jealousy and wishing ill upon the other. What was left after the sudden vaporization of habitual negativity was nothing short of miraculous: a delicate, courteous loving-kindness toward one another that—despite a few setbacks when we were in our teens—has characterized our relationship ever since.

What we two had experienced, all unsuspecting, was grace. Though we were far too young to analyze what had gone wrong between us or who was to blame for it, and though we were still too immature to offer an apology to one another, deep inside we yearned for peace. That honest longing was all it took; God filled in the gaps for us, the gaps we were too young to negotiate on our own. Only now do I understand what a remarkable gift that sudden, unexpected reconciliation represented. Most of the time, forgiveness is not this unthinking or instantaneous. Instead, it is more often a complex, painful process, fraught as any novel with disappointments and reversals. "Forgiveness is the final form of love," says theologian Reinhold Niebuhr, but lest we mistakenly assume that because we love, we are natural-born forgivers, Gandhi adds this caution: "The weak can never forgive. Forgiveness is an attribute of the strong." Both of these twentieth-century social activists worked tirelessly for justice and human dignity. Neither of them doubted the reality of evil, much less took it lightly. Yet both believed that at the core of meaningful existence lies the terribly difficult task of forgiveness.

Why is forgiving such a challenge? From whichever perspective we approach it—whether we are trying to forgive someone who has hurt us, or are in dire need of forgiveness ourselves—when we enter into the process, we find ourselves laid bare. The intense searchlight of mercy invades our every hiding place. We cannot go through being stripped of false dignity and self-justifying excuses without being changed. Transformation is unavoidable, for our blind eyes have been opened and now we see.

In my own case, it was a vengeful dream in my late thirties that transformed me. A self-absorbed and unstable person was making my life miserable by spreading malicious gossip. I was becoming a little crazy over the whole situation. All I could think of was how to stop the onslaught of hateful words. My anger was understandable—even justifiable. Until I dreamed of murder, however, I had no idea of how dangerous it is to nurture rage. I was shocked at myself. I had always thought I was a good and decent person, an enlightened being who worked for justice and peace. This level of killing anger did not fit into my view of myself.

I was also shaken by another realization. It appeared that there was an ironic aspect to forgiveness—that we often bear more animosity toward someone we have harmed than toward someone who has harmed us. As Quaker Jessamyn West points out, it's easier to forgive others for the mistakes they make than for their witnessing our own, and this was certainly true in the case of my dream. The person who was tormenting me, the person I visualized shooting, was someone who had once admired me and wanted to be my friend. Though I was shocked by this realization and what it revealed about me, I had little idea of what to do about it now. At some level, I understood that taking its implications seriously would precipitate a major change in the way I saw the world, and this prospect was frightening. Despite my hidden shame, I preferred to keep things as they were; life was familiar this way, and I was comfortable with it.

Eventually, however, God reintroduced the issue. I was driving on a lonely stretch of the California coastal highway north of Santa Barbara, when suddenly, something barely visible in the deepening twilight began to materialize on the roadside ahead. I slowed to see better: it was a man dragging a large wooden cross, mounted on what looked like roller skate wheels.

I gaped at him for a moment, then flashed on by. Though I looked for him in my rearview mirror, he'd already been erased by the falling darkness. As it turned out—it was in the paper the next day—I'd seen a real man on a real pilgrimage heading up the coast of California, but that didn't diminish the eerie quality of the experience. The vision of myself as a heartless murderer seemed somehow linked to that dreamlike Christ figure struggling on through the twilight.

When, some time later, I felt myself being inexorably turned by God in a whole new direction, the same two images rose before me like a pair of somber icons, gleaming with mysterious significance in the light of my new faith. On one hand was self-styled payback, so ugly but so satisfying, and on the other was perfect love, the kind that could finally heal my angry, wounded, guilty heart.

Though I was sincerely appalled at the violent emotions revealed by my dream, it was only after my reconversion to Christianity that I began to question my automatically hostile responses to other people's hostility. I couldn't get away with "doing what comes naturally" any longer. Becoming a follower of Christ requires that we give up what feels normal and enter uncharted and mysterious new territory. Christ requires a radical change of direction, and he models a way of being in the world that often brings us into shocking conflict with our notions about what it means to be a decent human being.

One of Jesus' most mind-boggling declarations, repeated throughout the Gospels, is that we who hope to follow him must first be willing to forgive the people who have hurt us. Not only does this injunction show up at the heart of the prayer he offers to his disciples ("Give us this day our daily bread; and forgive us our debts as we forgive our debtors"), but he restates it as a requirement for salvation: "If you forgive others their transgressions, your heavenly Father will forgive you. But if you do not forgive others, neither will your Father forgive your transgressions" (Mt. 6:11–15).

He also tells us that if we wish to live in relationship with God, we must first seek forgiveness from those we've hurt: "Therefore, if you bring your gift to the altar, and there recall that your brother has anything against you, leave your gift there at the altar, go first and be reconciled with your brother, and then come and offer your gift" (Mt. 5:23–24). Our damaged relationships with other people, especially when we are responsible for that damage, have a direct effect on our friendship with God. We cannot pray with any kind of integrity while blithely ignoring the fact that we've wounded another person. Jesus tells us that we must first take care of business—make amends and do our best to reconcile—before we approach our Father in heaven.

By the time God tracked me down in the wilderness, I'd been wandering alone for years and was more than ready to come home. Yet something kept holding me back. It was only when I began to reexamine my hidden hostility toward anyone who crossed me that I saw what it might be: my refusal to forgive was an unmistakable sign I was not yet ready to obey God. And if I could not, for love of him, give up my own will when it came to grudges, then who was I kidding? I might "believe" in an intellectual sense, but that was a dangerous illusion. To truly believe in God without loving him, as Jesuit Marko Rupnik points out, is impossible.

Why is it so difficult to forgive? What is it about being forgiven that secretly galls us? Why couldn't I admit how much guilt lay concealed beneath my coldness toward a would-be friend? *Forgiveness: Following Jesus into Radical Loving* has evolved out of my attempt to answer these questions. Since I was only able to start seeking and offering forgiveness when I started to take Christianity seriously, I have confined myself to that viewpoint throughout these pages. But there is a more important reason I've chosen to talk about forgiveness from the Christian perspective: I've slowly become convinced that the centrality of forgiveness in Christianity is unique among the great religions and philosophies of the world, peace-loving Buddhists included.

Why? No other religion came into being through an act of forgiveness. Without God's merciful and forgiving love toward his creatures, there would have been no Incarnation, and thus, no Christianity at all. Christ became man in order to rescue us from the ravages of sin and restore us to spiritual health. The success of his ongoing redemptive project, which is to be carried out by his children on Earth, depends before anything else upon our realizing that we are in serious need of forgiveness.

As Christ puts it, "Those who are well do not need a physician, but the sick do. Go and learn the meaning of the words, 'I desire mercy, not sacrifice.' I did not come to call the righteous but sinners" (Mt. 9:12–13). His mission is to make whole what has been fragmented, damaged, or destroyed through the depredations of evil. Yet only we who are willing to acknowledge our own spiritual illness are open to this kind of healing.

In other words, we must first undergo redemption ourselves—a redemption that begins with the experience of being forgiven—before we are ready to join in Christ's work of reclaiming what has been lost to sin, death, and the power of the devil. Only then can we become participants in the great project of transforming evil into good.

Father forgive

On a moonlit night in 1940, at the height of World War II, 450 German bombers dropped five hundred tons of high explosives and forty thousand fire bombs on a single British city.

Over fourteen hundred people in Coventry were woefully injured or killed. Among the many buildings hit during the massive attack was the graceful St. Michael's Cathedral, founded in the twelfth century and rebuilt beginning in 1373. At the end of the Luftwaffe raid, which lasted eleven hours, only the outer walls and spire of the eight-hundred-year-old church remained standing.

While a stonemason was picking through the smoking debris of the church the next morning, he found two blackened oak beams lying across one another in the rough shape of a cross; he tied them together and set them in a barrel. A priest fashioned a second cross from three medieval nails. These two crosses would eventually become international symbols of reconciliation. But before that could happen, the people of Coventry would have to deal with the fact that their lives had been changed forever. Not only had they lost friends and relatives in this unprecedented attack—the first in history launched with the goal of destroying a whole city in a single air raid—but in many cases they had also lost their homes, their sources of livelihood, and their hope for the future. Before they could even think of forgiveness, the people of Coventry would have to deal with their terrible grief and rage.

In the days following the bombing, the cathedral provost helped point the survivors away from their completely justifiable urge for retaliation and toward the ideal of loving the enemies who had destroyed their way of life. He mounted the stonemason's cross of beams above the charred altar and had two words carved into the red sandstone behind it: FATHER FORGIVE. Though his message of forgiveness was particularly controversial during this time of all-out war, his steadfast insistence on following Christ through the valley of grief and rage created an opening in Coventry for eventual healing and reconciliation.

When the cathedral was finally rebuilt, the new building was placed so as to face the ruins, the cross of beams, and the carved sign. The cross of medieval nails was placed on the altar inside the new modern church, one wall of which was a seventy-foot-high glass screen. When I stood inside that church a few years ago and looked out toward the grassy ruins, it took a moment to realize what I was seeing, faintly etched into the soaring glass that divides the new from the old. Superimposed against the sky, hovering over the bombed out cathedral, great flocks of angels, apostles, and prophets raised their hands toward heaven.

When Christ tells us we must take forgiveness seriously, he also promises to accompany us. We do not seek or offer forgiveness on our own; we cannot. It is only through him that we are able. Our role in forgiveness is far humbler than his. We are to bear the burden of our recalcitrant selves, slowly learning to shed the mass of fear and self-concern that blocks his work in us.

part 1
before we can forgive
intellectual impediments to forgiving

one forgiveness and
the problem of evil

I WAS SEVENTEEN before I experienced my first real doubt about God's existence. It did not come out of thin air. It was the summer of 1969, and I was living in the back room of an Alliance for Progress clinic in the mountains of Honduras with another girl my age. We were Amigos de las Americas volunteers, and our job was to inoculate as many people as we could against smallpox, tetanus, mumps, measles, and diphtheria. In the short time we'd been there, I'd already been brought face to face with more physical affliction than I'd seen during my entire life, and the magnitude of suffering was starting to give me nightmares.

Then, one morning, as Sue and I were standing at the examination table unwrapping needles we had sterilized in the pressure cooker the night before, someone began knocking on the heavy wooden door of the clinic. We were used to people coming by at all hours to ask for vitamins, cough medicine, and aspirin, and our inclination that morning was to pretend we hadn't heard—after all, we'd be opening up in less than twenty minutes, and whoever it was could certainly wait till then. Then the person at the door began to wail.

I went to the window and pushed open the wooden shutters. A woman stood on the front steps, a dirty towel over her head and a bundle of rags in her arms. The moment she saw me looking down at her, she went silent. But she stared back at me with fierce concentration, as though I were a doctor—as though I knew what to do.

"Open the door, Sue," I said. "I think it's a baby."

Inside the foul mound of rags lay a wizened little creature who turned out to be a girl. I couldn't tell her age. She looked far older than a newborn, though she couldn't have weighed more than seven or eight pounds and her skeletal limbs were wrinkled with dehydration. The mother was murmuring in Spanish, explaining that this child had dysentery and was very hot, couldn't eat, couldn't suck, was clearly dying. She pointed to the half-open eyelids and the half-moons of white that gleamed beneath them.

Sue and I had some medical training and had been issued a good medical book besides, so we had some inkling about what we could try: we could mix sugar and salt with water and put it in a syringe for oral feedings every ten minutes. Maybe—who knew?—it would help. It certainly couldn't make things any worse. We prepared the first syringe, and Sue began dropping fluid into the baby's mouth.

Meanwhile, people were lining up for their shots on the dirt road outside the clinic. We put the woman and her daughter in a chair in the corner, and checked on them in between inoculations, making sure the oral feedings were taking place on schedule. By the time the mother trudged off in the evening, her child's eyes were focusing. It had been an all-day vigil to save a baby whose odds of survival were already ridiculously low in this malnourished, poverty-stricken place. Sometime during those hours, doubt had started forming up in me.

Who was God, after all? If he was both all-good and all-powerful, as I'd always been taught, then why didn't he *do* something about this sad place? Did his apparent absence mean he didn't love us as much as we hoped? Or was he really not omnipotent after all, and simply incapable of coping with the world as it was?

I couldn't bear these thoughts—if I were going to believe in God, then I wanted him to be the one I knew from the Bible, the one who lovingly kept track of sparrows and cared about every hair on my head. In light of how unjust I was discovering the world to be, what possible good was an ineffectual, disconnected deity? Wouldn't it be better for us to simply tackle things ourselves, as we'd done with this dying baby?

My youthful protest at the apparent injustice of God soon hardened into a cynical agnosticism that set my course for nearly twenty years. When, in the 1980s, villages like the one I'd lived in were systematically destroyed by government death squads in Guatemala, El Salvador, Nicaragua, and southern Mexico, I kept thinking about that baby and all the children like her—the "throwaway" children who were quietly expiring by the thousands before they ever had a chance to live. My midlife reencounter with God, no matter how gratifying, did not immediately resolve these questions about injustice and evil. I still wanted some answers I could live with. How could you forgive evil and still fight for what was right?

challenges to Christian forgiveness

Simon Wiesenthal, a Jewish concentration camp survivor who spent his life tracking down and identifying Nazi war criminals, writes about the uneasy relationship between evil and forgiveness in his book *The Sunflower*. While still a prisoner, he was put on a work detail that took him to a Red Cross hospital. There he was approached by a nurse, who asked him to follow her to a room in which he found a dying SS soldier. The man wished to confess a terrible atrocity he committed under Nazi command—helping to pack a house with hundreds of Jewish men, women, and children, and then torching it. He desperately needed forgiveness, and he begged Wiesenthal to grant it to him.

Wiesenthal could not—but he spent the rest of his life in conflict over his decision. At the end of his book, he asks, what would you have done in my place? A number of famous contributors are invited to write essays in response. The majority agree: no forgiveness is possible in this case. Their primary reason for rejecting forgiveness as an option is a particularly powerful one, and has to do with fear of perpetuating evil. In order to prevent us from ever again going through a moral catastrophe on the scale of the Holocaust, they say, the blood of the innocent must continue to cry out forever. We must *never* forget—and forgiving assures that we will.

Only a handful of writers—all of them, with the exception of the Dalai Lama, are Christian—see things differently. For them, forgiveness is not only appropriate, but an urgent necessity. Why? They agree that we must do everything we can to prevent another massive outbreak of evil on the scale of Hitler's genocide. But they disagree about how we best handle that threat. The radical Christian belief is that evil is only overcome when it is transformed into good. Much of the evil in the world will not be truly overcome, but the possibility exists that it *can* be, and we cannot afford to miss the opportunity when it presents itself. Forgiveness is a key aspect of this very mysterious and transformative process.

Yet even those of us who accept the Christian view go through a struggle when the crime seems particularly heinous. In the fall of 2006, the Old Order Amish of Nickel Mines in Lancaster County, Pennsylvania, suffered a tragedy that momentarily rocked the nation. On a lovely fall day, a non-Amish neighbor of the community, Charles Roberts, drove to a nearby one-room schoolhouse, ordered all the boys and adults out of the classroom, nailed shut the doors and drew the blinds, then tied up ten little Amish girls whom he planned to molest—in retaliation, as he put it in his suicide note, for God's allowing his infant daughter to die years before. However, the police arrived almost immediately. Instead of carrying through with his plan, Roberts shot the girls execution style, and then turned the gun on himself.

Three girls died at the scene, and two others, both from the same family, passed away hours apart in separate hospitals. The five remaining victims were critically injured. The community, shocked and grief-stricken, surrounded the bereft families with love and kindness. They also went to the widow and parents of the killer and offered their sympathy and support within hours of the shooting. They told the relatives of the man who had murdered their children that they forgave him and bore him no ill will. They made it clear that they wanted to continue their longtime neighborly relations with the family.

Though the swiftness of the Nickel Mines Amish to forgive a man who had just executed their elementary school–age daughters was both astonishing and admirable, for many people it was also deeply troubling. Why?

One of our great modern legacies, for good or for ill, is a passionate devotion to the self. A beneficial side effect of this self-absorption has been a greater respect for individual life, and possibly even an increased capacity for empathy. Because we ourselves feel that we can demand respect simply by virtue of being alive, we are willing to extend that respect to other people. When we see human dignity being egregiously violated, we become outraged.

When the scale of violation is overwhelming, as in the Nickel Mines episode, or too monstrous to comprehend, as in the Holocaust, the Rwanda genocide, and the systematic destruction of villages in Central America during the 1980s, we are overwhelmed with sympathetic fury. We feel that to speak of forgiveness in such circumstances is to engage in the grossest kind of disrespect toward innocent victims. Forgiving the perpetrators of such evil means that we offer our sympathy to the very people who have been merciless toward others. What about the demands of justice in such circumstances?

the requirement of truth

Those who work on international truth and reconciliation commissions have a clear picture of the depth and range of evil in the world. Listening to story after story of cruel atrocities committed against often innocent people takes both courage and the hope that somehow, despite the horrors they have undergone or caused, victim and perpetrator can be reconciled and go on to live in peace. Interestingly, what victims often want from their oppressors before anything else is not so much a sign of repentance or apology, but the *truth*—no matter how grisly—of exactly what happened. They want to be released from the hell of perpetual wondering. The moment they hear this truth, no matter how it shatters them, is the moment that opens them to the possibility of forgiveness.

Thus, forgiveness cannot ever require that evil be overlooked, explained away, or excused; if it is, evil will certainly grow and flourish. An aspect of justice is that the truth be revealed; another aspect of justice that we often prefer to forget about, as

South African theologian Charles Villa-Vicencio points out, is that every perpetrator, no matter how savagely he behaves, is also a human being. The Christian belief in original sin suggests that, given the right combination of circumstances, we are *all* capable of unspeakable deeds. When we turn perpetrators into monsters, we deny this common ground between us. According to Villa-Vicencio, it is unjust not to acknowledge this basic fact of our shared propensity for evil.

It is certainly true that some crimes against humanity are so unthinkable they can never be legally redressed. It is also true that some wounds never heal, especially those that occur after a sustained, deliberate attempt to strip us of our humanity. The philosopher Simone Weil says that cruelty on this scale can lead to a soul-killing condition she calls "affliction," which is to be distinguished from simple suffering.

Yet Christianity still insists that forgiveness can serve as an "outward and visible sign" of Christ's redemptive presence. Even here, forgiveness can insure that evil does not have the last word.

blaming God for evil

Not everyone is convinced by Christianity's bold assertions, however. My teenaged anger toward God for his seeming injustice in Honduras was not only perfectly understandable, it is the main reason many people simply cannot believe, no matter how they try, in a good and all-powerful God who is intimately involved in the world. They feel we would do better to let go of our lofty theistic notions and get on with dealing with what is here.

The writer Albert Camus takes up this old argument in his 1947 novel *The Plague*. The protagonist, Dr. Bernard Rieux, lives in the Algerian city of Oran, where thousands of rats suddenly begin dying in the streets. He immediately suspects an outbreak of bubonic plague, though his suspicions are ignored by the authorities. Soon, however, people begin dropping dead, and the city is sealed off from the world. The story revolves around the characters' responses to an unexpected, catastrophic event. Opportunists figure out how to make money.

The local priest uses the epidemic to launch a moral diatribe against his lax parishioners. And Dr. Rieux works tirelessly to save whomever he can, despite the utter hopelessness of the situation and despite his already pronounced weariness with life. The work gives him no rewards whatsoever, but he doggedly continues to do it and thus wrings a kind of nobility out of a meaningless situation.

For many years, I chose the course laid out by Camus. I would work for good, I told myself, and forget about trying to please this nebulous thing called God. Instead of reading the Bible, I read the great atheistic existentialists such as Jean-Paul Sartre, who did not claim to know anything much at all, and certainly nothing about God, in whom he did not believe. He advised that we simply try to live "authentically" in a universe that—with all its tragedy and woes—could not but seem absurd to thinking, feeling creatures like us. Taking life on the concrete level, detached from any lofty attempts to make it more than it was, made sense to me.

Ironically enough, however, one of the main reasons I finally returned to Christianity was *because* of its robust stand against evil. As my own life grew increasingly complicated and filled with responsibilities to others—responsibilities I was often failing to meet—the existentialist refusal to recognize any moral givens wore exceedingly thin. Not only did it offer no way to become better, it could not even offer reasons to be good. But coming back to Christianity meant once more having to grapple with that old, frustrating question: why would a good God permit evil?

The answer I was taught in Lutheran Sunday school, usually referred to as the free will theory, asserts that God—desiring sons and daughters, not automatons—gave humans the ability to freely choose or reject him. St. Augustine, a proponent of this belief, says that the best possible universe will obviously contain free-willed, rational, moral beings—though this free will unfortunately means that some people may choose to embrace evil. Since God has allowed us to freely choose what we will do, however, it is not fair to blame him for the results.

Theological explanations such as this one are called theodicies; they are attempts to justify and explain why God does what he does. The philosopher Alvin Plantinga, in his book *God, Freedom, and Evil,* analyzes a more modest argument, one he calls the free will defense. Instead of purporting to know what God's reasons for permitting evil *are,* we should say what they *might possibly be.* And one thing we can suggest is that there might be some kind of good—one we cannot imagine—that even God cannot bring about without permitting evil.

A human analogy for this theological problem might be the dilemma in William Styron's famous novel, *Sophie's Choice.* Here, a Polish woman unfairly accused of collaborating against the Third Reich is arrested by the Gestapo and sent with her two young children to Auschwitz. At the gates she is confronted by a sadistic guard who offers her a deal. Both children are destined for the gas chamber, he explains, but he, in his kindness, will spare one of them. She has to choose which one that will be. Her wrenching decision, which leaves her with unbearable guilt for the rest of her life, results in unintended and unwilled evil: the death of her beloved little girl. To save her daughter, however, would mean the death of her son. In this case, there is no way to do good without a corresponding evil result. God's decision to create human beings in his own image, with the freedom to either accept or reject his love, was a wonderfully good act that nevertheless opened up the possibility of evil in the world.

The free will defense is perhaps the most convincing explanation of the coexistence of God and evil. I must admit, however, that I, like most other nonphilosophers, am not deeply moved by philosophical arguments, even powerful and impressive ones like Plantinga's. The problem of evil continued to impede my growth in faith, and it was only when I had to confront the results of my own self-centeredness—only when I looked into the mirror and recognized a great sinner—that the Christian story and its version of the relationship between God and evil started to make sense to me.

Christianity asserts that we are made to love God, and when we choose ourselves over him, we choose an anxious half-life that leaves us defenseless against opportunistic evil. Despite our stubborn resistance, God sends us a savior to help us out of this trap of our own making. However, instead of being grateful for the rescue attempt, we crucify him and go on in our self-absorbed way. Without Christ, however, not only are we incapable of loving God, we cannot possibly love one another on the scale required. It is easier to focus on our private lives and personal relationships and let the rest go. The resulting indifference to our fellow human beings is the real cause of most suffering in the world.

I did not want to face this fact, not as an idealistic young teenager and not as a perpetually outraged adult activist. I wanted to blame someone at the top for the misery and distress that seemed to characterize most human lives. Yet what I was seeing when I looked into the cloudy eyes of that woefully dehydrated baby was the natural result of millennia of human sinning.

On the subject of our neglected neighbors, Christ is characteristically blunt. Despite what we profess to believe, without loving actions toward one another, we cannot qualify as his true followers. As Jesus' own Jewish tradition would put it, we are to be God's hands and feet in the world, and if we don't do the work he puts before us, who will? He tells us that what we do for the least of our brothers, we do for him. He explains that when we feed the hungry, extend hospitality to the homeless, clothe the naked, care for the sick, and visit those in prison, we show him love at the same time. And when we turn our faces away from those who are hurting or in need, we turn our faces from him, too (Mt. 25:31–45).

With these words, Jesus calls us to something more than simply resisting sin. He calls us to succor the victims of evil, both the moral evil so obviously caused by human beings and what is often referred to as "natural evil"—the catastrophes unleashed by earthquakes, floods, droughts, and disease—the effects of which are so often compounded by human wrongdoing (witness Hurricane Katrina). It seems that we are indeed meant to be our brother's keeper, and in every act of love for that brother, we also, mysteriously, love Christ.

discerning the face of Jesus

Even though these words of Jesus are likely familiar, we are still startled and amazed when people take them seriously. The person who lives out these words often becomes a saint. Francis of Assisi famously kissed a leper; Mother Teresa pulled the homeless and starving out of the gutters of Calcutta so that they could die with dignity; Sister Helen Prejean ministers to brutal murderers. We can't fathom such selflessness; we assume special gifts must be involved because normal people are incapable of such acts.

Yet Jesus calmly states that *all* of us, no matter how imperfect, are meant to live this way. We are to love one another as Jesus loves us. We cannot live only for ourselves and still call ourselves Christian. The radical individualism of the twenty-first century makes it especially difficult for us to grasp, much less begin to live by, this outrageous concept.

Christ's injunction to forgive only begins to make sense when we read it in this context. If we have not yet gotten the point, if we don't yet understand what a truly radical form of love we have been called to, then we will never get past our sense of self-righteous affront at the all-too-obvious sins of everyone around us. We will be tempted to take up the cause for social justice, write scathing diatribes, even donate money, all the while doggedly avoiding the face of Christ next door.

Forgiveness as Jesus teaches it in the Gospels is the natural extension of his wider teaching on love. The Amish, who seemed sincerely puzzled at the astonishment of the media over their ability to forgive, tried to explain that forgiveness is simply a manifestation (sometimes, as in this particular case, a dramatic one) of a life lived according to Christ's double commandment of love: "You shall love the Lord your God with all your heart, with all your soul, with all your mind, and with all your strength . . . [and] you shall love your neighbor as yourself" (Mk. 12:30–31). The fact that the Amish could forgive when they were so grievously injured does not imply that forgiving is any easier for them than it is for us—only that they are fully convinced that Jesus' teachings on forgiveness lie at the heart of what it means to be a Christian.

None of this, when I first began to figure it out, was welcome news. The double commandment of love and Christ's injunction to forgive clearly had major implications for the way I lived my life, and I didn't yet feel ready to accept and act on them. But no matter how I scanned the Gospels for a loophole, or even one good reason to stall a little longer, I kept coming up empty-handed.

two forgiveness and
   the problem of justice

WHILE I WAS STILL in that village in Honduras, pondering God's apparent neglect of the suffering, one of the program route drivers showed up with a pickup truck full of supplies and a batch of letters from home. I tore open the one from my boyfriend and devoured it on the spot, then looked fondly over the envelopes from various family members. They could wait—first we had to unload.

Sue and I chatted with Jorge while we helped him move boxes of worm medicine and vaccine from the truck into the clinic. How were things going in the other villages? What was the news from the States?

One volunteer had dysentery, he informed us, but she was being treated. Mostly, things were good. However, something very bad had happened in America—hard to explain. Jorge kept moving boxes without saying more.

"What?" I asked him finally, filled with trepidation. "What's the bad thing that is hard to explain?"

"People were killed," he told me reluctantly. "A pregnant woman—a movie star—and others, too. People came in and destroyed a millionaire's house and everybody in it," he went on. Nobody knew why.

He shook his head and grew quiet. I looked at Sue and she looked at me. We had no way to get news from home except by letter or emergency telegrams. Nobody had mentioned something like this. I decided Jorge had gotten it wrong. It didn't make any sense, for one thing. Who did things like that? Who caused random chaos? I felt chilled, as though touched by the breath of evil. It wasn't until I got back to Southern California that I heard the story of the Manson murders.

Though Charles Manson and his gang were eventually rounded up and put in prison, their drug-fueled spree came to symbolize the dark side of American life in the sixties. They were in some ways the final straw for a society already fed up with massive antiwar protests led by long-haired flower children. Law and order became the rallying cry for the 1972 political election, and the self-designated law and order candidate, Richard Nixon, won hands down.

America's demand for justice at the end of a tumultuous and in many ways frightening decade was completely understandable. One mark of a civilized society is peaceful orderliness, and the Manson murders seemed to be evidence that things had become too lenient. Society can't function when we feel that everything is out of control; when we begin to sense chaos looming, our unfortunate tendency is to rush toward anyone who promises to contain further disruption.

Good laws help prevent this frightened rush toward demagogues who either promise what they can't deliver or strip us of our rights in the name of order. Jesus never suggests laying aside good civil or religious laws: "Do not think that I have come to abolish the law or the prophets. I have not come to abolish but to fulfill. Amen, I say to you, until heaven and earth pass away, not the smallest letter or the smallest part of a letter will pass from the law, until all things have taken place" (Mt. 5:17–18). The law is meant to teach us and guide us, to provide a kind of trellis that will help anchor us while we learn to handle our spiritual freedom. As such, good laws are as necessary to the religious life as they are to a civil society.

How, then, does forgiveness preserve either kind of law? How can someone like Charles Roberts, murderer of Amish schoolgirls, be forgiven, if it means that he might escape just punishment? Is it possible to both punish and forgive an offender at the same time?

the two kingdoms

One answer—the belief that the Amish subscribe to—is that forgiveness and pardon most often take place in different realms and involve different sets of values. These two realms are what Jesus calls the kingdom of God or heaven, and the kingdom of the world. Jesus makes a clear distinction between what his followers owe to one realm, versus what they owe to the other. When the chief priests and scribes try to trick Jesus by asking him whether or not it is lawful for religious Jews to pay tribute to Caesar, he says, "Show me a denarius; whose image and name does it bear?" They reply, "Caesar's." So he says to them, "Then repay to Caesar what belongs to Caesar and to God what belongs to God" (Lk. 20:23–26). Here Jesus disabuses us of the notion that the principles and practicalities of earthly government are a direct analogue for how things work under the reign of God.

In Luke, chapter 12, for example, he advises his followers to settle their differences outside of court—through forgiveness and, if possible, reconciliation—because once they go before a judge, they are subject to the values of the kingdom of the world (civil law and all its penalties). Jesus never suggests that these penalties are not proper and fair—only that it is wiser for his disciples, who are on a spiritual path, to avoid getting caught up in a system meant for the world rather than for the kingdom of God.

His point in these two lessons is that we can't expect one kingdom's set of values to work in the other. Christ holds the Pharisees and scribes to a much higher standard than he does others, primarily because they are representatives of the kingdom of God, meant to help further the spiritual lives of their people. His expectations for those in the world, on the other hand, seem both realistic and pragmatic. Those who do not follow him are going to think differently, solve problems differently, and even sin differently. They are going to employ legal punishment to keep order, for example.

Forgiving is an act that takes place in the kingdom of heaven. Pardoning, on the other hand, has more to do with the kingdom of the world, particularly the legal system. In forgiving, we may voluntarily forego our right to vengeance and deliberately let go of anger and hatred toward our victimizer. Yet we do not necessarily pardon the one who has wronged us—in fact, that decision usually is not even up to us. The person who has hurt us must often accept the legal consequences of his or her actions, which may mean years of punishment of one sort of another. None of this, however, precludes forgiveness.

Where we really get ourselves into spiritual trouble over the law, according to Jesus, is not when we forgive but when we cave in to the temptation of valuing personal righteousness over a developed capacity for mercy. Using the Pharisees as an example of how blind adherence to the letter of the law not only misses the point but can cause us to become morally deformed, hateful people, Jesus says: "Woe to you Pharisees! You pay tithes of mint and of rue and of every garden herb, but you pay no attention to judgment and to love for God. These you should have done, without overlooking the others" (Lk. 11:42). In other words, when it comes to obeying the law, our actions are important, but our motivations even more so. We cannot satisfy the requirements of the law if our reasons for doing so are actually sinful. For example, when we wield the law to bolster our own reputations, we actually condemn ourselves: "You justify yourselves in the sight of others, but God knows your hearts; for what is of human esteem is an abomination in the sight of God" (Lk. 16:15). Even if we manage to manipulate others through our false righteousness, we can't fool God; he knows who we are and why we do what we do.

The law is meant to be our guide, not our god. It is meant to be an arrow that points us toward the goal: the gradual development of a Christlike character within us. As we grow in the virtues that Jesus modeled—prudence, justice, fortitude, temperance, humility, faith, hope, and love—we are increasingly able to handle the hard times that eventually come our way. More, we can strengthen and inspire those who are suffering, discouraged, or in despair. Our obvious peacefulness and inner joy become a blessing and a light in a world that too often seems overwhelmingly danger-ous or hopeless. Disguised within the law, including the Ten Commandments, are these

beautiful virtues of Jesus, which are also meant
to be ours. When, on the other hand, we allow
ourselves to become obsessed with "measuring
up," or when we get sidetracked by egotistic
self-righteousness, we miss the point entirely,
and thus squander the gift.

Christ's development of the law

Jesus' attitude toward the law comes into better
focus when we place it within a historical context.
He arrived in the midst of a society firmly rooted
in the notion of fair play. Much of Mosaic law, as
it is worked out in Exodus, sounds quite similar
to older Mesopotamian codices: the Late Period
Egyptian codes based on the concept of Ma'at,
for example, or the codex of Ur-Nammu, King
of Ur (2050 BC), or the Code of Hammurabi
of Babylon (1760 BC). All are meant to settle
conflicts and help people avoid continual strife,
and most insist that the indigent—particularly
widows and orphans—not be oppressed, and
slaves not be killed with impunity.

Despite similarities to other ancient codices,
Mosaic law, delivered by God himself to Moses

on Mount Sinai, represents an advance over earlier conceptions of justice. For example, where Egyptian law might imprison whole families for the crime of a father or brother, Mosaic law does not punish vicariously. Where the Hittite laws of restitution require that a stolen ox be repaid with ten, Mosaic law is less harsh: five will suffice.

In other words, we are not to profit by being victims, but when we are hurt, we should be willing to accept fair recompense. Rather than demand more than is equitable, we are to "give life for life, eye for eye, tooth for tooth, hand for hand, foot for foot, burn for burn, wound for wound, stripe for stripe" (Ex. 21:24–25). Though such stark accounting may sound harsh by modern standards, to accept what is fair without caving to the temptation of revenge is actually a form of humility. In Mosaic law, justice ultimately rests in God's hands; humility is the much-valued Hebrew virtue of knowing one's place before an almighty God.

Jesus takes this admirable Hebrew system of justice and internalizes it—writing its wisdom on the heart, as he puts it. Obedience to external laws becomes the silent, interior impulse of a new kind of character, the basis of which is an even more profound form of humility than that already practiced by the Jews. "You have heard that it was said, 'An eye for an eye and a tooth for a tooth.' But I say to you, offer no resistance to one who is evil. When someone strikes you on [your] right cheek, turn the other one to him as well. If anyone wants to go to law with you over your tunic, hand him your cloak as well. Should anyone press you into service for one mile, go with him for two miles. Give to the one who asks of you, and do not turn your back on one who wants to borrow" (Mt. 5:38–42). It is difficult enough to stop ourselves from hitting back harder than we've been hit, but according to Christ, we are called to go beyond what is merely difficult to what seems nearly impossible: returning good for evil.

Jesus differs even more profoundly from the larger, pan-Mediterranean world of which he was a part, which during his time still operated on a code of ethics derived from the ancient Homeric warrior society. In this kind of shame-and-honor system, we strive to live up to the expectations of our social group rather than those of God, and we accept the group's judgment on our worth. We are justifiably proud of our courage, loyalty, strength, and nobility, and our shame is great when we fail. If someone declines to show us proper respect, he must be called to account or we lose face. If someone harms a friend or family member, vengeance is not only permitted but required. Under this view, humility is not remotely a virtue but instead a sign of baseness. Peasants and women are humble; warriors and true aristocrats are proud.

For example, in the war poem the *Iliad*, which recounts Greek events that take place at roughly the same time as the Exodus, the great hero Achilleus becomes excessively offended at a public slight and withdraws his forces from a battle with the Trojans. When his best friend, Patroklos, is killed by the Trojan hero Hektor, however, both honor and guilty grief require that he return to the fray. However, it is not enough to merely slay Hektor in revenge; Achilleus goes on to desecrate his body, and only ends the vengeance ritual when Hektor's aged father comes to plead for mercy.

Socrates, Plato, and Aristotle built their ethical systems on the venerable foundations of this ancient tradition, but they internalized the standard. Socrates, for example, teaches that a man's real judge is himself, and that self-respect trumps popular acclaim. A man who knows himself, and who has striven to be virtuous, is not affected by pubic misunderstanding. During his famous death scene in Plato's *Apology*, Socrates sums up his philosophy: "A good man cannot be harmed, either in life or death." His strength and dignity, however, are not rooted in humility but pride. Through intense self-discipline, he has transcended the baseness of the average man.

In regard to the vengeance cycle that is so much a part of the Mediterranean world of his time, Jesus says, "You have heard that it was said, 'You shall love your neighbor and hate your enemy.' But I say to you, love your enemies and pray for those who persecute you that you may be children of your heavenly Father, for he makes his sun rise on the bad and the good, and causes rain to fall on the just and unjust" (Mt. 5:43–45). With his words from the cross— "Father, forgive them, they know not what they do" (Lk. 23:34)—he demonstrates through the suffering of his own flesh that, no matter how excruciating it may be to offer merciful love to an oppressor, the vengeance cycle can only be broken in one way: through humility.

our elevation of self

After two thousand years we have not made great progress in the direction Jesus indicated. Though we have taken some wonderful strides in the areas of human rights and social justice, our culture is still in large part driven by values derived from both Mosaic law and the Greek honor code. To a far greater extent than the Hebrews did, we expect fair play and just compensation, and we are willing to go to court to fight for them. To protect the people we cherish, we are too easily swayed by leaders and others seeking our approval when they promise that criminals and other wrongdoers will pay for their crimes with the modern version of an eye for an eye. And, like the Greeks and the Trojans, we are more than willing to make war.

If Mosaic law and the vengeance cycle are still alive and well, where in our Judeo-Christian culture do we find the influence of Jesus' teachings regarding justice? We can certainly find traces in our high regard for the individual person. Jesus' valuing of the human person over strict adherence to the letter of the law is illustrated in the story of the woman caught in adultery. Though the crowd is ready to stone the woman for her sin, Jesus stops them in the act by issuing a simple challenge: "Let the one among you who is without sin be the first to throw a stone at her" (Jn. 8:7). Strict enforcement of the law may protect social order, but according to Jesus, an individual soul—sinful and complicated though it may be—is far more precious in God's eyes. Our concern for the rights of the accused is evidence of the extent to which these teachings have permeated our cultural mindset. We presume that people are innocent until proven guilty, and we are willing to provide public defenders for those who cannot afford legal representation. Even though our society has sometimes disregarded the dignity of persons, we are quite aware that we fail morally when we do so.

Our elevation of the individual has by now been mostly disconnected from its original spiritual root. However, it would be difficult to find a Christian idea that has had a more significant impact on our culture. We believe we are entitled to respect simply because we exist, without any need to earn it through our exploits on behalf of the community, as Achilleus had to do. And we are convinced that the most important thing we can instill in our children is self-esteem—that private, satisfying sense that we are fine and important people with a multitude of gifts to share with the world. Thus, one of our primary goals is to achieve a life that is worthy of who we are. In this milieu, Christ's injunction to forgive is even harder to obey than it was in ancient days. We simply don't know how to deal with wounds that damage self-esteem.

the uniqueness of Christian forgiveness

Though Jesus' teachings certainly help elevate the status of the individual person, the notion of self-*esteem*—the idea that we can and should hold ourselves in high regard, apart from anybody else's opinion—is a modern one that did not exist during his day. Christ's valuing of the individual human person was revolutionary in a clan-based society, where one's public role rather than one's unique personality defined one's identity, but self-esteem as we know it was not part of the early Christian view.

Much of what we believe about the self today comes to us through psychology and its focus on the mysterious world within. It seems that who we are cannot be fully explained by our social roles. There is a personal, private side to human existence that is deeply affected by life experience. And our development can be stunted when such negative or traumatic experiences lead to self-hatred. As a way to counteract a negative self-image, educators and psychotherapists have tried to foster self-esteem, a robust love and admiration for the self that does not depend on our achievements or our virtues. We are to love and respect ourselves as we are, no matter what; our esteem for ourselves must be unconditional.

Few would dispute the assertion that a healthy sense of self is a good thing. However, an unquestioning commitment to modern notions about self-esteem can make it impossible for us to comprehend the religious point of view. When the moral weight of our actions is disregarded for the sake of maintaining unconditional self-esteem, for example, we lose the ability to see ourselves as sinners in need of salvation and transformation. We assume that we are fine the way we are, and that those who use the language of sin and redemption are being dangerously judgmental. When self-esteem is our primary goal, we learn to see ourselves and our own concerns as ultimate; we lose our sense of awe in the face of the divine.

During the Last Supper, Jesus talks about the requirements of discipleship in ways that challenge our ingrained notions about self-esteem. First, he says, only those of his followers who are humbly aware of their true relationship to God will be able to do anything worthwhile for him, no matter how gifted they may be. There is no place in God's divine project for the prima donna or the superstar. To continue carrying out his great works once he has ascended to the Father, Jesus explains that what he needs from his disciples is the acquiescence of humility: "I am the vine, you are the branches. Whoever remains in me and I in him will bear much fruit, because without me you can do nothing" (Jn. 15:5). Yet our elevation of self-esteem to the status of a primary value more often than not precludes this deep humility called for by Jesus.

Second, those who want to work for God must be capable of obeying the many moral and spiritual injunctions God has given them, including the Ten Commandments, the Beatitudes, and the lessons Jesus imbedded in the parables. This call to obedience is not simply an exercise in authoritarianism or a test of loyalty. Hidden within the commandments and parables are the seeds of a new kind of character, one that is holy and partakes of the divine. To be holy is to be free of the downward drag of sin that occurs when we organize life around placating every desire or acquiescing to every passion, no matter how base. This freedom from the constant demands of the self opens our hearts and allows us to live more lovingly and courageously. Trusting Christ, we surrender to his care our burden of anxious concerns and responsibilities, and thus begin to experience true, deep joy and a "peace that passes understanding."

The first step in transforming the old, blind, sinful self into this new, sanctified person is to honor God's authority, regardless of how unnatural it might feel to do so. And it *will* feel unnatural, for another hallmark of Western culture is our stubborn unwillingness to live under authority. We are proud of our democratic way of life and become outraged when we suspect we're being coerced or manipulated by those in charge. We resist hierarchy of any kind, and we

firmly believe that real men (and women) bow
their knee to no one. To obey is to admit that
there is someone wiser and better than we are,
and this is a hard admission to make for people
steeped in a culture of self-esteem. Yet obeying
even when it feels unnatural is also a marvelous
exercise in trustful letting go. Just as it can be a
great relief to turn the steering wheel over to our
spouse when we're exhausted from negotiating
crazy traffic, so it can be an enormous release to
say, "I trust you, Lord, and if you are telling me
to do something, I know it will be good for me."
Jesus sums up what this trustful surrender really
means in very simple terms: "If you love me,
you will keep my commandments" (Jn. 14:15).
However, for we who are convinced that the
path to self-fulfillment lies in following our own
noses, Jesus' call for self-denying obedience is a
particularly difficult one to take up.

The third thing Christ tells his disciples they
must be able to do is recognize truth. Though
on their own they are incapable of discerning
wisely, he tells them he will send the Holy Spirit
to teach them discernment. Their job is to cling

tightly to what the Holy Spirit reveals to them, and not to get sidetracked by their own selfish desires, for self-centeredness will shutter their vision: "And I will ask the Father, and he will give you another Advocate to be with you always, the Spirit of truth, which the world cannot accept, because it neither sees nor knows it. But you know it, because it remains with you and will be in you" (Jn. 14:16–17). For us modern individualists, Jesus' pointing toward an absolute truth that supersedes all others again raises the specter of authority—this time an intellectual and spiritual authority—that we can't help but resist in our stubborn self-sufficiency.

Finally, those who want to serve Christ must serve each other. They must become as cooperatively interdependent as parts of the same body, for they are to become the living manifestations of Christ for the rest of the world: "I give you a new commandment: love one another. As I have loved you, so you should love one another. This is how all will know you are my disciples, if you have love for one another" (Jn. 13:34–35). Once again, Jesus puts it very simply: they will know we are Christians by our love. C.S. Lewis insists that we are almost never converted through logic but instead "infected" by a love that moves us so powerfully we can't help but succumb. A modern spiritual writer, Donald Nichols, reiterates the central importance of love to evangelization when he refers to the "theology of faces," or the look of love that says everything about the faith behind it. Our society, however, is characterized instead by its hyperindividualism and its intense need for "personal space" and privacy. We feel that we are doing well simply by avoiding conflict. The notion of actually loving one another sounds either idealistic or uncomfortably communal. We much prefer our separateness, even as Christians—hence our many sects and denominations.

But according to Christ, only those who find and cling to the virtues of humility, obedience, wisdom, and love can be used by God for his redemptive work in the world. Jesus models this path himself, relying on God for everything and taking no personal credit for the great miracles he performs: "The words that I speak to you I do not speak on my own. The Father who dwells in me is doing his works" (Jn. 14:10). Meeting someone who actually lives by these countercultural values can be an overwhelming experience. The first time I visited the hermitage where I eventually became a Camaldolese Benedictine oblate, I was struck by the gentleness, kindness, and anonymous hospitality of many of the monks. The older monks in particular, who had lived in community for many years, had clearly had their sharp edges rubbed off by a way of life that is meant to foster obedience, humility, spiritual wisdom, and love. What took longer for me to notice, however, was how much spiritual power lay hidden beneath their gentle exteriors. Jesus transforms us for a reason; only when we are willing to put the demanding ego under authority is it safe for us to handle this kind of power.

He also straightforwardly acknowledges that our road will not be easy: "If you belonged to the world, the world would love its own; but because you do not belong to the world, and I have chosen you out of the world, the world hates you" (Jn. 15:19). He is so concerned about the dangers his followers will face that he prays to God for their protection: "I do not ask that you take them out of the world but that you keep them from the evil one" (Jn. 17:15). Yet the pressure to conform to the values of popular culture makes us feel extremely uneasy about the possibility of being despised for our beliefs. How often is being "liked" more important to us than living with integrity?

But Christ's disciples are called to do one thing and one thing alone—continue the work he began—and this is what gives purpose and meaning to their lives, no matter how difficult or dangerous our course might be. We are like brave little ships, setting out upon a stormy sea, and he worries about us as a parent worries about his children. It is through our lives that others will find their way home: "I pray not only for them, but also for those who will believe in me through their word, so that they may all be one, as you, Father, are in me and I in you, that they also may be in us, that the world may believe you sent me" (Jn. 17:20–21). Our focus on self-fulfillment, in contrast, may make us nervous in the face of this kind of dedication. Aren't we giving up too much—closing off options—when we throw our energy into one thing and one thing alone?

If we are only able to take it in, Christianity offers far more hope for humankind than our blind allegiance to individualism could ever allow. The prophet Isaiah, writing seven hundred years before the birth of Jesus, declares exultantly that under the rule of Immanuel, evil shall not only be contained but utterly vanquished: "The wolf shall be a guest of the lamb, and the leopard shall lie down with the kid; the calf and the young lion shall browse together, with a little child to guide them. . . . The baby shall play by the cobra's den, and the child lay his hand on the adder's lair. There shall be no harm or ruin on all my holy mountain; for the earth shall be filled with the knowledge of the Lord, as water covers the sea" (Isa. 11:6, 8–9). Given the world we live in, it's easy to dismiss this beautiful vision as idealistic fantasy, but we catch glimpses of this realm all the time. Whenever Christians come

forward in the midst of turmoil, offering hope
and love, they introduce people caught up in
rage or terror or despair to their real identities as
human beings created in the image and likeness
of God, people who are inherently valuable in
the sight of Jesus. And this can be enough to
turn lions into lambs.

When Christians risk their own lives for the
sake of Christ and other people, they can stun
the world into thoughtful reflection about its
propensity for violence. For example, during
the Los Angeles riots of the early 1990s, truck
driver Reggie Denny was unmercifully beaten
by a brick-wielding mob. Four strangers heard
about what was happening on their radios and
immediately got into their cars and drove to the
scene. Despite the danger to themselves, they
rescued Denny, dragged him into his truck, and
got him to a hospital, where his life was saved.
When asked how they'd been able to overcome
their own fear in order to offer this act of love,
their reply was simple: We're Christians. How
could we not? In St. John's revelatory vision of
the "new heaven and the new earth," enemies

will not simply cease destroying one another; they will embrace: "Behold, God's dwelling is with the human race. He will dwell with them and they will be his people, and God himself will always be with them [as their God]. He will wipe every tear from their eyes, and there shall be no more death or mourning, wailing or pain, [for] the old order has passed away" (Rev. 21:3–4). Though, once again, such an idyllic future may seem like a woefully naïve hope given the circumstances under which we live, Jesus himself gave us the first glimpse of how things could be when from the cross he forgave his executioners. And Christians throughout the generations have found their inspiration for countless deeds of self-sacrifice and forgiveness in this hope for ultimate peace. From the first martyr, St. Stephen, who prayed that those who were stoning him would not be punished, to the modern-day mother who adopted the young murderer of her only son, Jesus' followers have put their faith in the possibility of a reconciled creation.

If any of this is to come to pass, however, the coiled serpent that keeps unblinking watch in every human heart must first meet and surrender to a power greater than itself. Evil is conquered and transformed on a heart-by-heart basis. And one of the most powerful weapons in this struggle is the simple but often excruciatingly difficult act of forgiveness.

part 2
preparing
ourselves to forgive

getting to know ourselves and
what impedes God's work in us

three the evil
I do not wish to do

I WISH I COULD SAY that the thought of murder, even in a dream, represented a complete departure from my normal state of mind, caused by a split-second loss of self under circumstances that would try the discipline of anyone. I wish I could say that no matter what sort of vigilante images my unruly unconscious had tossed up that night, they were not me. The person I am would never do such a thing, never consciously *think* such a thing. Something else, something not-me, was responsible for this abrupt and violent twist in my way of seeing the world. Something had momentarily taken me over. This, at least, was how I tried to reassure myself.

Then I began teaching a new class at the university, one that focused on nineteenth-century novels and novellas. Dostoevsky's *Notes from the Underground,* a first-person narrative by an anonymous and thoroughly despicable character my students dubbed the "U-Man," wound up on my syllabus. The opening lines set the tone for the whole work: "I am a sick man. . . . I am a spiteful man. I am an unattractive man. I think my liver is diseased." I had someone read the words out loud. The class snorted and rolled their eyes. I told them to spend five minutes writing about the similarities between themselves and the U-Man, based on these few lines. They groaned, and someone—the reader—flung his pen dramatically to the floor.

"Are you telling me," I asked them, "that there's *nothing* in this guy you can relate to? Nothing whatsoever?"

A thoughtful look came over their faces. The reader scooped up his pen and began to tap his forehead. There was a sustained, collective sigh, some shuffling of feet and rearranging of paper. Then they settled down to write. I watched them affectionately for a minute, then realized who was leaving herself out of the exercise: me.

How was *I* like the underground man? In what ways was *I* spiteful, unattractive, sick in my dealings with others? I pulled my journal from my backpack and, without thinking about the ramifications of what I was about to do, began to record whatever came to me. Ten minutes later, we looked up at each other, dazed. "Whoa," said the reader, fanning his face with spread fingers.

"Who wants to share?" I asked.

In the back row, where on too many days of the week a group of hungover students slouched, a hand went tentatively into the air. "Yes?" I said.

"Well," said the student, his voice gravelly from so rarely being used in a classroom, "I'm pretty sure my liver's shot by now." He glanced up sadly at the chorus of appreciative snorts that followed this announcement. "No, really," he said. "I'm not kidding."

The room went silent. People were looking at the floor, their journals, the palms of their hands—anywhere but at the young alcoholic, now so nakedly exposed, still slouching in the back row. Without a clue about what to say next, I cleared my throat and started to speak. But before I could get a word out, another hand went up. "I'll go," said a young woman. And proceeded to read to thirty of her peers a lengthy list of what could only be called sins.

The session that followed was one of the more remarkable classroom experiences I have ever had. One by one, these self-assured young people, normally so pleased with themselves, revealed their darkest and most primitive urges, their nastiest habits, their secret envies and hatreds. At the end of the hour, we shuffled out the door without my having had a chance to close off the session with any teacherly words of wisdom. I *had* no words of wisdom. We'd just gone through a communal confession, and I'd come to see that we were all in the same boat, those students and I.

This, in fact, was Dostoevsky's great insight about human nature, which he wrote about in novel after famous novel. He saw that in every heart there exists a "slinking whisper," as the Muslims would put it, a sly, persuasive voice that tells us we are good when we are not and convinces us we're acting rightly when we're wrong. This is the nature of temptation—it is an insidious line of internal chatter that works to make us proud of what's worst in us. Uncovering the worm at the core, especially in the cathartic way it had just happened in that classroom, can be shocking.

But it can also be freeing. For as Jesus assures us, when we know the truth, we will be free, and one of the most basic truths, however unwelcome it might be, is this universal truth about the lie we tell ourselves.

the nature of the lie

Why are we so susceptible to this kind of self-deception?

In his classic explication of faith, *Mere Christianity*, C.S. Lewis offers a possible explanation. He begins by pointing out that most human beings, regardless of culture or religion, seem to be born with an innate sense of right and wrong. Though every society comes up with its own take on what constitutes the good (our contemporary—and, I believe, mistaken— notion of cultural relativism stems from this undisputed fact), no society believes it is okay to do wrong once the parameters have been defined.

For centuries, Lewis says, this curious, inborn ability to tell right from wrong was referred to as the "law of nature," and it traditionally constituted our common ground as human beings. Under this view, we might disagree from culture to culture about which specific acts are good and which ones are bad, but we never disagree about the notion that people should try their best to aim for good acts.

More, when we do choose what we know to be wrong, it generally isn't because we want to *be* bad but because we believe the badness will somehow lead to good. For example, as a nation, we're unlikely to go to war for the pleasure of killing people and destroying other countries.

Instead, we go to war because we have become convinced, whether rightly or wrongly, that we are setting out to defend what is good.

Even the very worst among us seem bound by this need to justify their acts, often working out elaborate rationales for the most horrendous cruelties. Hitler asserted that his "final solution" was the only way to purify a once-great but now polluted Aryan race. Stalin assured himself that his mass murders were giving the glorious communist experiment a chance of succeeding. In our day, radical Islamic imams who convince young people to become suicide bombers are careful to stake their moral authority on words from the Qur'an, even though these have been taken out of context.

Under this view, it's conceivable that depraved sexual predators or serial killers commit their crimes not for the joy of being evil, but because the acts somehow make them feel good—offering a kind of twisted pleasure, or the illusion of being in control of a frighteningly chaotic existence, or a conviction that they are on some kind of holy mission.

It seems that we can be deeply mistaken about which ways of being in the world are *truly* good, but it would be extremely rare that someone deliberately chooses to do evil for its own sake. Even the half-crazed, vengeful monster in Mary Shelley's *Frankenstein* is careful to make this distinction when he tries to justify his many murders to a sympathetic listener: "Evil thenceforth became my *good*."

The strong demand we place on ourselves to measure up to a standard of goodness seems to contradict the popular contemporary view that we can't help how we are. Despite what psychoanalytic theory puts forth regarding the irresistible power of the unconscious, or what geneticists tell us about inherited brain chemistry and how it drives us, we continue to act in ways that reveal our true belief: as people passionately devoted to the development and flourishing of the self, we are firmly wedded, whether we recognize this or not, to the Christian concept of free will—the conviction that we are capable of making real choices about what we do and who we are.

A difficult problem comes packaged with this moral freedom of ours. Even though we accept the law of nature as right and true, says Lewis, most of the time, we don't keep it. And since we are fully aware of our failure to meet the standard, we feel ashamed. As in the days of Homer's warriors, shame is the stomach-dropping realization that we have let ourselves down before others in such a way that we may never recover our standing. We have been judged as seriously deficient, and we accept that judgment as true.

Shame before God involves the same set of emotions, minus the hopeful possibility that we can somehow make things right again through our own efforts. Unless we have already experienced his merciful and forgiving love—unless we know the difference between genuine humility and abject shame—we tend to become paralyzed under these circumstances. How can we ever meet God's standards, given that he is the source of all goodness? The fact is, we cannot; and when we let this sink in, it's easy to despair, for shame can be truly unbearable. We'll do almost anything to avoid experiencing it.

One handy shame-avoidance technique is to twist the facts in such a way that we can continue to do what we want without having to pay the price. We tell ourselves a story that exonerates or even elevates us, despite our wrongdoing. When, as a young married woman, I first found myself falling in love with another man, I was so afraid of what might happen to my marriage, and so ashamed of myself for my disloyalty, that I could not even think rationally about what was happening. Instead, day after day, I poured out my heart in my journal. Without ever referring directly to what was going on, I wrote about how starved I was for a creative outlet, how miscast I was in the role of homemaker and wife, and what a mistake I'd made in getting married so young. I turned myself into a marital version of the poor little match girl, cheated through no fault of her own of everything that would make life meaningful.

Had real-life consequences not finally intervened, I could have spent the rest of my life embellishing this sad tale. For what begins as a simple lie to avoid shame often evolves into a novel-like life story with convincing subplots that explain every twist and turn in our path. The villains in this narrative are those who call our essential goodness into question. As we delve deeper into the self-justifying story, we begin to see other people not as themselves but only in relation to how willingly they affirm the conclusions we've drawn about life. They become fictional characters, no longer separate persons with their own complex histories and intelligences.

A second method for avoiding shame, a particularly popular one today, is to banish it altogether. We decide we are done with such a painful and burdensome emotion, and we refuse to buckle under it anymore. But we can't successfully get rid of it without first rejecting the standard that convicts us, so we declare that everything is relative, including right and wrong. We profess to believe that good and evil are not real, but simply terms for what people happen to personally like or dislike. And we certainly can't be blamed if something we do morally displeases someone else—that's their problem, not ours.

However, we cannot so easily escape our inbuilt knowledge of right and wrong. According to the philosopher Immanuel Kant, it is our moral sense that distinguishes us from other creatures and marks us out as human. Like it or not, we are stuck with our moral selves, which means we are forced to continually deal with the threat of shame. And despite our sophisticated intellectualizing, we can't seem to run fast enough to avoid it. Shame, a twisted and abject version of the holy humility to which Jesus calls us, seems to be our contemporary human lot.

the emergence theory of evil

Environmentalist David Bella sheds light on our complicated relationship to shame and the disastrous consequences it can engender in his essay on contemporary emergence theory. He believes that, despite the way they are caricatured in horror movies, most scientists whose technological breakthroughs wind up leading to environmental destruction or moral catastrophe do not begin as "evil geniuses," bent on controlling the earth. What fuels their energetic research and development is often nothing more than intellectual curiosity and the understandable desire for respect and recognition from colleagues.

He tells the story of a young Kazakh scientist who was offered the opportunity to direct a major Soviet secret research facility. Given that his field—biology—was so competitive, it was an honor to be chosen, especially given his age and lack of experience. The added factor of total secrecy made the offer all the more intriguing and reflected back on him as someone not only competent but trustworthy at the highest level.

Motivated by the strong desire to prove himself, he took the job. Even when it became clear that he would be overseeing the development of biological weapons of mass destruction, he found himself so deeply committed to demonstrating his competence that he could not bring himself to withdraw. Instead, he told himself a series of stories: I am not in charge here; I don't make the ultimate decisions; I am only doing my job in the best way I can; I have already sworn myself to secrecy and cannot be disloyal to the state.

In the emergence theory of evil, disaster on a grand scale usually does not begin with a single decision on the part of some powerful person, but instead with a series of individual choices that have to do with proving oneself and avoiding shame. As political philosopher Hannah Arendt notes in her classic "report on the banality of evil" in *Eichmann in Jerusalem* (1963), what is often most shocking about those who commit the greatest crimes against humanity is their bland normality. Adolph Eichmann, on trial for the murder of millions of European Jews, was, astonishingly enough, still prone to bragging about his promotions within the Nazi hierarchy. Even as he contemplated execution or life imprisonment for his unimaginable crimes, he cherished the memory of his successes within the organization. For him, as for most of us, those successes were what held the specter of shame at bay.

Does the emergence theory help shed any light on the spiritual journey? Early Christian writers might say yes. They believed that our ultimate orientation, whether for God or for evil, was not necessarily the result of a one-time decision—a born-again experience, as some might call it today—but rather was the culmination of a number of smaller choices. We might choose Christ, be baptized, and embrace the spiritual path with every good intention, but still find ourselves in peril.

The Catholic teachings on mortal sin as a severing of the relationship with God that must be sacramentally repaired, are built on this original notion that the Christian life is a path on which we will meet dangerous and even spiritually deadly obstacles. This sense of precariousness permeates ancient Christian thinking and helps account for an intense focus on achieving *puritas corditas,* a heart so pure that it is no longer burdened by the need to look good at any cost.

Purity of heart means that every desire is for the same thing: God. Does this imply that other loves are wrong, or other goods illusory? No. The Christian view has never been a traditionally stoic one; we are never meant to deny or totally overcome our passions and desires. Instead, purity of heart refers to that joyful state of being in which we can freely love the good things of life while never losing sight of our North Star.

Achieving purity of heart, however, can be the work of a lifetime. Along the way, we are still apt to mistake the strong desire to *feel* that we are good for the state of actually *being* good. Whatever bolsters our sense of rightness or competence or giftedness or popularity can easily become part of the evidence we so desperately seek.

Thomas Merton's spiritual autobiography, *The Seven Storey Mountain,* offers a classic example of the struggle it can be to sort out the difference. Though Merton honestly longed for purity of heart, he never knew for sure what was driving him. Before his conversion to Catholicism in his twenties, he'd already attracted the attention of the New York literary scene. Once he entered the Trappist monastery of Gethsemane to become a monk, he was worried that continuing to write would draw him back into his old longing for artistic acclaim. Yet he had an important story to tell—the story of a young man in the sophisticated twentieth century once again discovering the ancient Christian path. So he wrote his autobiography, which quickly became a bestseller and inspired a whole new generation to enter monastic life.

Merton did not doubt that God was using his gift; what continued to weigh on him the more famous he became was whether he himself was acting out of pure motives or was still being secretly driven by that old vainglory. Neither his fame as a writer nor his growing influence as a spiritual mentor could settle the issue for him. Eventually he realized that it was being faithful to the anonymous, daily discipline of monastic life that held the best possibility of purifying his heart. For being faithful to his practice meant making thousands of small decisions to continue putting God first in his life. The moment he allowed himself to be distracted by other things, no matter how worthy or good, he started to lose his bearings.

As in David Bella's environmental model, our choices for lesser goods—for example, competence in our chosen field, social approval, an unimpeachable reputation, a happy family life, even peaceful relationships with others—can ultimately overwhelm the most fervent commitment to Christianity. The combined weight of these perfectly respectable decisions inexorably bends our spiritual trajectory. At the end of the day, we may be shocked to realize that we have spent most of our time and energy shoring up self-esteem, not living for Christ. What we devote ourselves to, in other words, ultimately defines us.

the genesis of the self-deceiving lie

The need to know ourselves as good, which Christianity would say flows from our being made in the image of God, can be perverted. The *imago dei* within us acts as a mirror that reflects back what we'd rather not see: our confused, insignificant, tiny selves, suddenly and vulnerably exposed in the radiant light of the divine. Shamed, we gasp and cover our eyes. Then we tell ourselves a story that explains away what we've just glimpsed, the first installment in what will become a legendary tale of who we really are, despite all evidence to the contrary. And we become furious with anyone who questions our self-serving self-assessment.

C.S. Lewis says that this huffy sense of affront, especially when it becomes chronic, is a strong indicator of incipient pride, the sin through which the "devil became the devil." This is the sin that can permanently harden our hearts against God, even those of us who sincerely profess belief. "Unchastity, anger, greed, drunkenness, and all that," Lewis warns, "are mere fleabites in comparison." For pride demands that we stop listening to anything but that slinking whisper that assures us of our infallibility and moral superiority, no matter what we do.

When we've reached this point, lying to ourselves about other things is not only easy, it is inevitable. For if pride is the sin of the devil, the devil is "the father of lies" (Jn. 8:44). And when we live in self-deception, we are wide open to temptation. Losing touch with the truth means losing our moral and spiritual compass. We can be conned by anything that promises to enhance our artificially enhanced view of ourselves.

God's merciful response to human failing

Interestingly enough, the very first story in the Bible has to do with this human stake in being good and the ease with which we are thereby tempted into pride. Adam and Eve's decision to disobey God in order to do what they wish introduces them to shame, which they find unbearable. So when they hear God calling to them in the twilit Garden, they resort to desperate lying, laced with self-justifying excuses that are intended to reestablish self-regard.

"It is not my fault," says Adam. "The woman talked me into it."

"It's not my fault either," she says. "I was tricked by the serpent."

The Old Testament is in one sense a long record of broken promises, violated trust, disobedience, and brother-against-brother violence. God's response to all this moral failure is striking. He gives his people a rule for life—the laws of the Ten Commandments—which they regularly disregard. Yet over and over again, God meets sin with love in the form of mercy.

One of the many threads that link the Old and New Testaments is this surprising gift of undeserved grace at times when strict justice would demand punishment. For example, Joseph, the favored son of Jacob, is sold to Egyptian slave traders by his jealous brothers. He survives and becomes the right-hand man of the pharaoh. A famine strikes Israel. Suddenly, Joseph's brothers show up in Egypt, desperately seeking food. They beg their former victim, who now holds life-and-death power over them, to please "forgive the crime that we, the servants of your father's God, committed" (Gen. 50:17). They stake their plea on the hope that Joseph is still a believing Hebrew, one who himself relies on the mercy and forgiveness of God. The strategy is a canny one. No real Hebrew can argue that God himself is not extravagantly merciful.

Neither can we. Our deepest sense of shame comes when we compare our habitual judgmentalism to God's seemingly endless willingness to forgive. Our foot-stamping demands for perfect justice look petty in the light of his merciful love. And so Joseph forgives the brothers who once wanted him dead. He seeks to obey the God who in Hosea 6:6 declares, "For it is love that I desire, not sacrifice, and knowledge of God rather than holocausts."

Throughout the Old Testament, God is characterized by this mercy coupled with justice. Numbers 14:18, for example, declares that "the Lord is slow to anger and rich in kindness, forgiving wickedness and crime." When God passes before Moses in the cleft of the rock, God cries out, "The Lord, the Lord, a merciful and gracious God, slow to anger and rich in kindness and fidelity, continuing his kindness for a thousand generations, and forgiving wickedness and crime and sin; yet not declaring the guilty guiltless, but punishing children and grandchildren to the third and fourth generation for their fathers' wickedness" (Ex. 34:6–7). In Psalms 86:5, the psalmist says, "Lord, you are kind and forgiving, most loving to all who call on you."

Jesus' teachings never deviate from this view of God as essentially loving and merciful in his role as divine judge. Jesus tells his disciples to "be merciful, just as [also] your Father is merciful" (Lk. 6:36). To be merciful toward others requires honesty, patience, and hope. First, we need to honestly face the facts—our uncle is an out-of-control alcoholic who is likely to kill someone on the highway, or our sister's chronic depression has encouraged her to become self-dramatizing and manipulative, or we ourselves are overly driven by ambition. If we don't, we're tempted to ignore or excuse what needs changing. Second, we must learn to be patient. When people change, they usually change slowly and in response to encouragement rather than harsh criticism. Patience also counteracts our temptation to draw permanent conclusions from present behavior. Finally, we must cling to the great theological virtue of hope. God loves our uncle and our sister and us more than we can fathom, and he can work miracles. Our mercy may actually be essential to his secret, transforming work. We cannot know the future, but we can trust in his goodness.

Jesus does not promise a world without conflict—in fact, families will be torn in two between those who believe in him and those who do not—but he tells his followers that they must consistently set aside their urge toward vengeance. They are to love one another, which means they are to patiently bear one another's failings without hatred and rancor. This is another way of describing mercy. And mercy is the root of forgiveness. The Eastern Orthodox Church sings of Christ during Easter Vigil that "on that day He shattered the sting of death." Jesus came to free us from more than one kind of death; among other things, he came to deliver us from our soul-killing bondage to shame and the prideful self-deception it generates—the self-protective stance that prevents us from opening our hearts to God and our fellow human beings. His extravagant act of forgiveness from the cross is meant to be our hope and our example. And when we truly desire to follow him down this difficult path of forgiving, he promises to bestow on us the strength we will surely need.

four telling the difference
between a real hurt
and a wounded ego

DOSTOEVSKY'S INSIGHT about the universal need for mercy and forgiveness helped me think in a new way about the people in my life who made me angry or hurt me in some significant way. I realized that I often refused to think of them as real people. Instead, I turned them into a kind of malevolent force, bent on thwarting me. If I hated the way I became in such circumstances, it was *their* fault, not mine.

I didn't want to be this way anymore. But Dostoevsky had shown me that I had no way to even think about forgiving them unless I first allowed them their humanity. To do this, however, I had to first give up a peculiar form of comfort I got from exaggerating their wrongdoing. The fact was, the worse they seemed, the better I felt about myself. The point where I could throw up my hands entirely—what on earth *motivated* such creatures?—was the pinnacle in terms of self-satisfaction. For it was here that the unbridgeable difference between us was most dramatically highlighted. *I* was good and *they* were bad. *I* was the victim, *they* were the oppressors.

Yet Dostoevsky had convinced me that my secret motives were often as nefarious as the next person's. When I was most convinced I was acting virtuously, I was often acting out of disguised self-interest instead. More, because of this tendency to view life in a way that insured I came out on top, my judgment was irredeemably flawed. Morally speaking, I couldn't see straight. Which must be why, it suddenly occurred to me, Christ warns us about judging others: "Stop judging that you may not be judged. For as you judge, so will you be judged, and the measure with which you measure will be measured out to you. Why do you notice the splinter in your

brother's eye, but do not perceive the wooden
beam in your own eye? . . . You hypocrite,
remove the wooden beam from your eye first;
then you will see clearly to remove the splinter
from your brother's eye" (Mt. 7:1–5). But how
do we even see that beam, I wondered, when
we're this blind?

self-centeredness as an obstacle
to good judgment

Early Christianity taught that good judgment
depends upon the same purity of heart that
fortifies us against the self-deceiving lie. The
moral and spiritual clear-sightedness that
allows for good judgment is known as *prudence*.
Without the ancient cardinal virtue of prudence
to guide us, we can turn other virtues into vices.
Imprudent courage can easily degenerate into
self-aggrandizing bravado, for example.

When we dominate our own landscape, the
shadow we cast is so huge it cuts the light by
which we morally see. Yet this tendency for the
self to hog center stage seems endemic to the

human condition. Our self-centeredness impairs our ability to make good judgments.

Buddhists consider the self and its private concerns so troublesome that they take truly radical measures against it. They insist that the self is nothing but an illusion that impedes our spiritual progress; the goal of Buddhist practice is to move past the concept of a separate self entirely. Yet the Buddhist eradication of the self as a way to purity of heart and clear vision, however impressive in its thoroughness, is not open to Christians.

Why? Because Christianity is inextricably linked to the strange but fascinating concept of personhood. A *person* in the religious sense is a creature with reasoning ability, a free will, a moral conscience, and a heart, or organ of prayer, that allows communion with the divine. More, a *person* is unique. The Orthodox point to Pentecost as the moment when humanity stepped into personhood. When the Holy Spirit descended in the form of separate flames that came to rest on individual heads, personhood was brought to life in us.

However, *unique* in the spiritual sense does not imply the same thing as *original* in the modern—which indicates that what we are has never been seen before. Instead, our uniqueness is the sign that we have been made by a loving and purposeful creator. We are not here by accident. We have been designed. We are meant for something. Our lives are inherently meaningful from conception onward.

Thus, denying the existence of the self cannot work for us as it can for Buddhists, even when it might allow us to circumvent ego and see more clearly. Under the Christian view, having a self is part of what it means to be a real person. The self, no matter how prone it is to sin, is the whole point.

Many philosophies and religions that preserve the concept of the self have, in fact, taken note of its tendency toward moral blindness and tried to diagnose the cause. Ancient Stoicism believed the source of our bad judgments is not the self per se, but emotions. Stoics like Epictetus believed that emotions are nothing more than wrong opinions, and we should either tightly control them or root them out entirely.

Not only Stoics, but also many Gnostics, Buddhists, and Hindus teach that suffering is caused by allowing ourselves to be driven by passion and desire. The solution to the human struggle is obvious: we must overcome emotional attachment of every kind, including, one would assume, our passionate stake in being good. We do this, they teach, by facing up to a basic reality about physical life: it is both fleeting and ephemeral. Nothing we do lasts; nothing we love survives death, so what is the point of worry or grieving? To counteract the human tendency to give in to the emotions, Epictetus urged his students to "watch over yourself like an enemy lying in wait." The only legitimate source of comfort for a real Stoic is to be found by contemplating an impersonal, orderly, and just universe.

The goal is a state of passionless serenity. This state, known in the Greek as *apatheia*, is more quickly reached when the physical world is taken as either gross and evil or as an alluring fantasy, one we need to grow past. Under this view, our deep longing for goodness, which can cause us suffering and which is vulnerable to perversion through self-regard, stems from a mistaken notion about our own importance.

Once again, however, Christianity sees things differently. Though Jesus never lays out his views about human passion and desire in any organized way, he demonstrates throughout the Gospels that the emotions (though they can be extremely troublesome) are not the deepest source of sin. He himself becomes angry at the money changers in the temple, speaks harshly to Peter when Peter tries to dissuade him from doing what he has to do, and weeps with Mary and Martha over the premature death of their brother Lazarus.

Therefore, when he makes what sounds like stoical statements, they cannot be read in the way that a Gnostic teacher or Hindu sannyasi would read them. These statements have another purpose; they are meant to redirect our emotional focus to what is most important. When Jesus tells us to let go of worry, for example, he's not saying we must force ourselves to overcome natural human anxiety about survival. Instead, he is pointing to an easily overlooked fact about being an adopted child of God, which is that we have direct access to the providence and loving care of "Abba."

Central to Christian teaching is the idea that we cannot blame the body for the evil we do. Body and soul are one in making the human person. However, in other traditions, the body with its urgent needs often takes the rap for our human propensity to approach life in self-serving ways. Ancient Gnostics repudiated the flesh as the source of our suffering, specifically our overwhelming fear of death and dissolution. Some Gnostics chose strict physical purity, lonely separation from the world, and a lifetime devoted to the interior journey as their solution. Others, known as antinomians, chose moral libertarianism. If they dissolved the moral standard, then whatever they chose to do was right—and they could at least enjoy themselves as they were waiting to die.

Even the classical Greeks, with their love of beautiful bodies, struggled with the issue of flesh versus spirit. In a famous Platonic dialogue called the *Phaedo*, Socrates converses with a couple of Pythagoreans about the body and its role in human life, referring to the flesh as "the prison of the soul." Early Christianity was much influenced by Platonic thought, and one often finds a similar rejection of the physical in Christian writing, especially during the Desert Father and medieval eras.

In the final analysis, Christianity says that our physical self can't be blamed for our inability to see straight. Though St. Paul refers to "the flesh" as a frustrating impediment to being good, Jesus never condemns either the body or any other aspect of the physical realm as a *direct* source of evil or bad judgment. Indeed, Christianity begins with the principle that the physical realm, created as it is by a loving God, is good in and of itself: "God saw how good it was" (Gen. 1:12).

Like all other good things, though, the body can be misused, mishandled, misdirected. St. Paul puts it thus: "Do you not know that your body is a temple of the Holy Spirit within you, whom you have from God, and that you are not your own? For you have been purchased at a price. Therefore, glorify God in your body" (1 Cor. 6:19–20). Our bodies do not belong to us; it is our obligation to be thankful for them and treat them with a certain degree of reverence.

how purity of heart intersects with forgiveness

If our capacity to make good judgments is impaired either through self-centeredness or habitual sin of whatever kind, we can't begin to discern what's really going on when someone appears to have hurt us. When we are romantically obsessed, for instance, we can't fairly or honestly assess the other person's response. His or her smallest gesture, no matter how insignificant, is mined for evidence of callousness. A careless word can trigger murderous, shame-based rage. I knew a woman who had been dating someone for several years and gradually became concerned, then angry, over the fact that he was not asking her to marry him. The more she brooded over why their relationship seemed to have stalled out, the more convinced she

became—despite a complete lack of evidence—
that he was still in love with his ex-girlfriend.
She began stalking him, and everything she saw,
no matter how innocuous, became part of the
case she was building. When he figured out what
was going on, he got frightened at her apparent
paranoia and ended the relationship abruptly.

An obsession with success can lead to similar
disastrous results. We become a walking time
bomb. Anyone who appears to impede our
progress is labeled an enemy. Whoever causes
us to fail or gets in our way is seen as a major
problem. My friend is a psychologist who coun-
sels a number of actors and artists. He finds
that in a highly competitive job market, these
creative people are particularly susceptible to
blaming others for their own failure to achieve
their goals: their problems, they believe, are the
fault of the publishers or the galleries or the
studios—rarely their own.

The sense of betrayal or deep hurt we harbor
when our vision is blinded by sin is an arrow
that points back to our own heart. It is a light
that reveals the hidden fetters that bind us to

false gods. We can't experience the liberation that comes with genuinely forgiving someone for hurting us if that sense of hurt has been generated by our own hypersensitive ego.

What feels like perfectly justifiable anger in these circumstances is often really spiteful-ness or envy or avarice in disguise. What feels like the pain of rejection is too many times overblown self-pity. When we habitually allow either the emotions or the yearnings of the body to dominate our thinking, we find ourselves enraged at perfectly innocent people. Piously "forgiving" them for what they haven't done is not the answer to our pain. In fact, it will make us hate them more.

In contrast, the ancient Christian hedge against a false sense of being hurt is the slow, gentle turning over of what is most urgent and demanding in us—our body's needs, our emotional obsessions—to God. In God, these overpowering passions are shown for what they are and thus brought down to size.

Despite what the old romantic manifesto, "I feel, therefore I am" tells us, we are far more than the sum total of our needs and wants and desires. And until we confront this basic Christian truth in a very personal way, we are not yet ready to forgive. We are still self-obsessed, and thus morally and spiritually blind. We may not even be able to tell the difference between what we imagine other people are doing and what they are actually up to.

a case of runaway ambition

Some years ago, I took a blow that rocked my universe: after three years of hard work on a novel for a major publisher, my contract was broken. This was not my first book. I began writing fiction when I was only seven, and the notion of becoming a great writer set my course. When I began publishing short stories at thirty, I thought I had it made.

But I was far from being a literary genius. And I was also far too bound up in family responsibility to write very much. First and foremost, I was by now a single mother of two young children.

Since I had no college degree and could qualify for nothing loftier, I was working two half-time clerical jobs on different college campuses. Most of the time, I was beyond exhaustion.

Yet I was so driven to succeed in my chosen field, that I'd start writing at 10:30 in the evening, after the kids were in bed, then try to juggle those two jobs the next day on only four hours of sleep. With that kind of price attached, my goal of becoming a famous writer became a quasi-religious ideal.

In time I married Mike, acquired two young stepdaughters, and went back to school to finish my degree. But all the way through, I clung tenaciously to the notion that I was meant for literary stardom. Even after a return to Christianity in my early forties, I kept my sights set firmly on the dream of literary success. And then I went to a writer's conference and was introduced to a famous agent. She agreed to read my work and take me on.

Within a few months, I sold my first novel to Random House as part of a two-book contract. On the day of publication, my editor shipped me an impressively hefty box of Godiva chocolates and a huge spray of red roses. The initial reviews were glowing, and everything seemed to be falling into place. I'd officially been "launched" in the world of the literati.

Inflated by grandiose visions of the future, I began novel number two. Since I was by now teaching full-time at the university and the four kids were all young adolescents, I was so busy I had to get up at 3:30 or 4:00 each morning to get my writing time in. But I was flying high on the adrenaline of self-assurance.

I shipped the book off a few days before deadline. It had been a tough project. I'd plunged deeply into both the politics and the dark religious crosscurrents in Guatemala and Mexico. It was a bit dangerous, I knew. Major publishing houses weren't known for their tolerance of religious subjects in fiction, but that didn't make a dent in my self-confidence. How could they not be *fascinated*? I thought to myself.

Jubilant and exhausted, I took a couple of days off work and headed up the coast to the hermitage in order to rest up and make a retreat.

Toward the end of the week, a monk knocked on my guestroom door with a message from home. My famous agent had called. She wanted to hear from me right away. It was urgent.

I finally got through to her on the monastery phone. The manuscript, she said, had lots of problems. *Lots*. She was almost positive my editor at Random House would feel the same. Maybe she'd be willing to roll up her sleeves and take it on, but probably not. I should be prepared.

I was stunned. But why? I asked. What's wrong with it?

My agent listed three or four fixable problems—I can fix them! I pitifully kept repeating—then zeroed in on the "religion thing." And there it was, finally out in the open, that which I'd secretly feared throughout the writing of the book. Though I hadn't wanted to admit it to myself, I'd had a strong hunch all along that I was playing with fire.

I should have *known* they couldn't handle my newfound religious sensibility, the one that had sneaked its way into an otherwise straight-ahead contemporary novel. But now she was admitting it out loud—the New York literary scene couldn't handle Christian novelists.

I was devastated, then outraged. This was prejudice, pure and simple, and more, it was utterly unfair. We had a *contract*. I'd *told* them what I was writing about.

Random House was just as thrilled with the new novel as my agent had been. In fact, my editor, when pressed, suggested I consign it to the Dumpster and start all over again. Again, I felt broadsided, then furious. And then, finally, bitter. I refused to even entertain the notion that there might actually be something wrong with the book itself. In my mind, this was all about my own victimhood.

Soon my hurt feelings morphed into something more complex: a somewhat paranoid story in which I was the misunderstood heroine and *they* were out to get me. Why? Because I was *brave* enough to take up a serious Christian faith in an era that despised it. (This part about my exceptional bravery was particularly satisfying, I found.)

Once the tale of my misunderstood heroism was fleshed out in all its details, it took on a power of its own. Suddenly, the everyday disappointments of university life—I didn't get this raise or that promotion—were weighted with new significance. I felt persecuted by people who'd once been my friends. I didn't fit anymore. So, at fifty, I quit and walked away from it all, in part because I couldn't bear myself in that setting any longer, though of course I would never admit *that*.

After a few months away, everything started to look different. Without the daily reminders of failure in an arena that had first seemed designed to showcase my success, I calmed down a little. I was still angry, true, but I was also starting to feel the pangs of conscience. After all, why carry a grudge this big into the future?

So I began the project of trying to forgive. I visualized everyone I believed had placed obstacles in my way. I prayed for them, pious "loving" prayers that asked God to show them their errors. But nothing happened. If anything, I grew angrier and more rigid in my bitterness.

I couldn't even think of these folks without getting a headache. And I thought—I have to let them go entirely.

Of all my misguided attempts at forgiveness during this trying time, this last was perhaps the wisest. The walking away, both emotionally and spiritually, gave me some open space in which to move on. It helped me stop obsessing about forgiving people I couldn't seem to forgive. It provided a healing interlude.

In that interlude—which went on for several years—I began to discern the truth of the matter. There *was* nobody to forgive. They'd all been acting within their understanding of what constituted integrity. They hadn't been "out to get me" at all. On the contrary, I'd no doubt caused at least some of them great puzzlement and grief. I'd been so aloof, so steely, so wounded. How could they have known what was going on with me?

The problem that had caused me so much distress was an internal one—in me, not them. It was born of an ego running rampant. I was suffering from ambition of the grossest kind—ambition that couldn't be thwarted in any way without a monumental, self-defensive reaction, out of proportion to the cause. They had innocently stepped into a snake pit of emotions having to do with my thwarted goal of universal acclaim. They hadn't set out to foil me. Instead, they'd been doing the best they could in the face of my mysterious persecution complex.

If anyone needed forgiveness, it was me, not them. First of all, from God, for transforming his gift to me—the ability to write—into an idol. And second, from my former friends and agent and editor for forcing them to take the blame for my ambition-fueled disappointment.

I stopped thinking about this whole mess as an unfinished forgiveness project and started working instead on learning to contain ambition. Something that proved helpful, if terrifying, was giving up writing altogether for a period of many months—a period purposely without an ending date. I needed to see just how much I was suffocating under the stranglehold of this idol. As I found out, quite a lot.

Being a writer—a famous writer—was so critical to my self-identity that giving it up, even temporarily, threw me into the murk of unknown territory. I found that I didn't know who I was when I wasn't writing. Was a wordless being worth anything at all? And if so, what?

That question took a while to answer. Meanwhile, I looked at my closest relationships and realized how often I begrudged time spent with people I loved simply because interacting with them took me away from my desk. Even more sobering, when I looked at the strangers who came and went in my life, I realized how ethereal they were to me. Completely absorbed in my writing as I was, they floated past me in ghostly insubstantiality, dissolving like smoke. Finally, I looked around for God and realized he'd made his quiet withdrawal some time ago without my ever noticing it.

No wonder I hadn't been able to "read" the situation with my publisher and agent for what it really was: their pragmatic response to the realities of the marketplace, not a personal attack on me and my faith. No wonder I couldn't discern what was up with my campus friends. I'd been utterly blinded by the god of ambition. And that god had managed to destroy a lot of good things in my life, some of which I truly cherished. What was I to do?

The Christian ascetical tradition helped save me from this mess. For it wasn't enough to simply stop writing. I had to get to know myself again. I had to ferret out what made me tick, then reset the clock. And one of the best ways to do this, I found, was by using some of the same methods the Desert Fathers had tried and found useful.

five disciplines as
        preparation for becoming
        a forgiving person

SEVERAL YEARS AFTER I QUIT my instructor's position at the university, I was invited to teach at a Christian arts and religion conference on the St. John's College campus in Santa Fe, New Mexico. Since I had always loved the classroom, I was happy to accept. Soon, however, I found myself trying to convince Mike that he really should come with me, even though there wouldn't be much for him to do during the time I was teaching. Something about doing this stint alone was making me nervous.

He agreed, and I relaxed a little. But when it came time to pack and actually get on the road, I again found myself behaving strangely.

Every time I looked around our little place in the country, I felt maudlin tears rising. It was so lovely, so quiet, so . . . idyllic. What on earth was I thinking? Why would a person ever want to leave such a place? (This, from a hard-core traveler.) Something seemed to be nailing my feet to the floor, and I was glad that we'd be on the road for a few days—it would give me time to calm down.

By the second night of the trip, we were only six hours away from Santa Fe. I crawled into the motel room bed and lay there, rigid and staring and . . . *what?* What was going *on* with me? My thoughts were not at all lining up with my feelings. What I was *thinking* was how glad I was to be invited to teach at this well-known conference. What I was *thinking* was that I'd been missing my old students, and that it would be great to meet some new ones. What I was *thinking* was that I was truly fortunate—indeed blessed—to be headed for such a beautiful place.

What I was *feeling*, however, was another story, and, at this point, completely untranslatable.

Whatever was going on in there, however, was serious business. My hands were clammy, my stomach felt punched, and all the muscles in my back were aching as though I were clenching them against imminent attack. The closest description I could come up with was a surprising one: my physical symptoms were the same you'd experience if you were suffering from an onslaught of icy terror.

My completely contradictory thoughts and emotions were a classic signal that Something Was Not Right Within. I truly believed that I was happy and excited about the teaching stint. I believed it so firmly—in fact, I repeated this nice thought to myself many times during the night—that I could not fathom why my feelings seemed so dramatically opposed.

However, as Jesuit Marko Rupnik notes in his book *Discernment,* a strong divergence between thoughts and feelings is a good indicator that we may be deceiving ourselves. In this case, the feelings are more likely to reveal our true orientation. And in my own case, they revealed an almost paralyzing fear of teaching at this conference.

Why? Once I let myself acknowledge this exaggerated and inexplicable terror, I could begin to sort out what might be causing it. The most obvious answer was that I'd left the university three years before under that burden of bitterness, and I hadn't been back in a classroom since. Would I wind up in the same boat? Would I feel that same sense of loneliness and isolation among my new colleagues? It made sense to me that at least some of this weird mental state could be attributed to reentering a university setting as a teacher.

But that couldn't possibly account for all of it. I slid out of bed, trying not to wake up Mike, who was sleeping off a long day of driving. Then I sneaked across the motel room floor and patted around in the dark for my bag. Somewhere in there was my journal and a pen. Once I got my hands on them, I slipped into the bathroom, snapped on the light, and sat cross-legged on the teeny shag rug beside the tub. Then I began to write.

What I discovered was that I truly wasn't afraid of teaching; I knew I was a good teacher and

I'd do a good job for the students. What I was afraid of was something else entirely, something having to do with that runaway ambition of the past. This might be a Christian conference, but the writers on the staff were literary writers, and the magazine that sponsored the event was a literary magazine. *Image* magazine had been launched, in fact, to provide a high-class venue for people like me, writers and artists who'd run up against the literati prejudice against too much religion.

No, what I feared was not my students or even myself as teacher; what I feared was that old demon of blind ambition, rising up in me again. For as part of this stint, I had to do a public reading, and the thought of an audience made me shiver. The notion of audience was what had driven me for years—people who would validate my greatness as an artist, people who would praise me and venerate my work. I had been so appalled years before when I figured this out about myself that I'd never wanted to be in that place of temptation again. And now here I was, six hours away from not only a classroom, but a stage. And the heels of my psyche were digging in hard, as if by keeping me immobilized, they could save me from great danger.

What broke the impasse was prayer. I said, "God, do you want me to go to this thing or not?" A voice inside of me—my own voice, but speaking firmly and with an authority I did not have—responded, "Yes. But right now, get back to bed and get some sleep," which I did.

This messy process, conducted in the middle of the night on a motel bathroom floor, was actually a form of spiritual discernment. My unacknowledged and exaggerated fear turned out to be an important cautionary message, courtesy of the Holy Spirit, which was that I needed to stay alert about the temptations toward ambition. I may have licked the enemy in one setting, but that did not at all insure he wouldn't come surging back in another, Christian or not. I was a fragile person in that regard, and probably always would be. For ambition had been a besetting sin for me, and our victories over besetting sins are—alas— often merely temporary.

The conference was, of course, wonderful, the students delightful, and the reading went pretty well, despite a deranged microphone episode that broke several eardrums, including my own. The biggest gift, however, was none of these, but instead, the revelation on the rug, one that I knew I must carry close to my heart, in order to *guard* my heart, forever.

Language like this—to guard, to be vigilant, to be alert—is the language of the Desert Fathers, who knew themselves better than most of us will ever know ourselves today.

the great experiment

The Desert Fathers and Mothers of the fourth and fifth centuries in Egypt and the Sinai were not just aiming to make a physical escape from the alluring distractions of big-city life. They were in part undergoing a new form of martyrdom that involved, among other things, the death of the grasping, acquiring part of the self. The hermits and monks who took up this life were involved in a grand experiment: how to discover their biggest obstacles to continuous communion with God, and then dismantle these. The experiment had to be adjusted depending on who was undergoing the struggle, for each person was complicated and, of course, unique and thus could be tempted in an endless variety of ways.

The tools of this experiment were spiritual disciplines or practices that forced one into a confrontation with the hidden sides of the self. Fasting, for example, very quickly unveiled incipient gluttony. Taking up voluntary poverty revealed tendencies toward hidden miserliness. The deliberate practice of patience twitched back the curtain on lurking arrogance and judgmentalism. Talking about such things in a theoretical way did nothing to change them. Even confession might help bring them into focus without actually curing them. The only solution was honesty, continual prayer, and an actual, physical shift in how one did things. The point was to slowly build new habits of thinking and acting. The Desert Fathers and Mothers were in many ways masters of psychology.

They were also more: they were spiritual athletes who understood that the covert operations of the self are what leave us wide open to the machinations of the devil. The ego's constant attempts to shore itself up and defend itself against shame are what make us vulnerable to Satan, an opportunist of the first degree. We need to know where these weak places are, identify them by name, pray for the grace to overcome them, and then—most important of all—take actual steps in the direction of change. If we leave off this last, we may understand a whole lot more about ourselves than we used to, but we'll probably keep on operating in a business-as-usual way.

good and bad habits

Simple habit, as Dostoevsky points out in his story of the underground man, is often the hidden factor in sin. Habits lead us in a particular direction. My habit of intense, daily writing for years, for example, led me to secretly believe and overtly behave as if the rest of life were secondary in importance. Habits create a structure for our lives, one that after long enough becomes what is "normal and natural." When we try to see past a habit-driven, ingrained way of thinking and acting, we either fail miserably or mistake that which is skewed for reality.

The great insight of the Desert Fathers was that habits that make us vulnerable to evil are only changed when we substitute habits that point us toward God and good. Thus, to counteract the tendency of isolated people to fall into romantic or sexual fantasy, they adopted the practice of vigils, or deliberately staying awake—keeping watch—throughout the night. To counteract avarice, they voluntarily gave away their possessions.

In my own case, it took reading about the Desert Fathers and their methods for changing habits to help me see what I'd been blind to for so long: both my thoughts and my behavior formed repetitious patterns. I reacted to life in certain ways not because those ways were particularly good or loving but because I was *used* to reacting like that. I began to think hard about these comfortable, familiar, and repetitious ways of thinking and acting and how they affected who I was as a human being, but this exercise quickly became overwhelming. The elders of the desert, however, were never in a rush. They knew that we would be spending our whole lives on this seemingly endless project of giving up the old, comfortable ways in order to make ourselves more available to God. If they could afford to focus on one problematic habit at a time, so could I. I decided to zero in on the obvious first: I talked about others far too much. Why was this "obvious"? Because more than one person—good friends, both of them—had (much to my chagrin) pointed it out to me.

This very bad habit of mine regularly manifested itself at dinnertime as Mike and I chatted about the day. I'd start by thinking about what I'd done and who I'd talked to, and pretty soon I was launched into a full-scale story about the (often hilarious) failings of somebody else. This made Mike laugh, which I found highly satisfying and took as encouragement to go on, but it was also sometimes cruel, or at the very least, unkind.

I realized that this habit of judgmental story-telling had nourished an attitude toward others that made it much harder for me to forgive them when I needed to. I couldn't stop seeing other people as *characters*—flawed yet fascinating characters—in a novel starring myself. Their little vanities and foibles interested me. I was intrigued by how often people seemed to have a picture of themselves that didn't match reality (naturally, I conveniently ignored my own recently revealed and pronounced tendency toward self-deception). I got a kick out of watching them strut around, completely unaware of how foolish and pathetic they looked.

When in real life I ran afoul of one of these characters, I felt that my previous negative or scornful judgment had just been confirmed. *Forgiving* such a person didn't cross my mind. It would ruin all the fun I had dissecting his or her personality at the dinner table each night.

Once I began to realize what arrogance lurked beneath this supposedly innocent storytelling habit of mine, and what an injustice I was doing to others, I began looking around rather desperately for a way to stop myself. The fourth-century desert monk Evagrius Ponticus, who seemed to have picked up some handy tips from ancient Greek medicine, recommends applying the antidote of opposition. If we have a problem with gluttony, for example, we should fast. If we have a problem with anger, we should do charitable works. If we have a problem with our tongue, we should maintain silence.

If not *constant* silence, I thought, at least silence during dinnertime when I was most tempted to regale my spouse with the perils of the day. So I tried holding my tongue the next night, and was immediately impressed by how *difficult* it was to give up this deceptively innocuous habit—harder than giving up sugar, harder than giving up sleep. Everything in me strained in one direction, the direction of the current great story I was having to sit on, while the remaining part—the puny part that was trying to do the right thing—struggled to head in the other.

What a lesson! In a single evening, much that had been hidden was revealed to me. The problem wasn't cured for a long time, and in fact, it's one I still have to battle. The moral of the story was obvious, however: to take up an ascetical practice for the purpose of transforming habitual thinking and behavior is truly a *discipline,* in the sense that it has to be worked at faithfully, prayerfully, and over a long period before we see any results.

An even bigger lesson, however, was the realization of how quickly we can cut through self-deception when we deliberately pit ourselves against our deeply ingrained habits of action and speech. In this sense, ascesis really is about getting to know the self. When we stop deceiving ourselves about who we are, we are better prepared to deal with the self-deception in others. This is why the Desert Fathers and Mothers so fervently practiced their disciplines. They knew what was happening invisibly inside them.

turning trouble on its head

The good news is that, under the logic of ascesis, everyday mortifications can also become life-transforming events. Instead of deliberately adopting a particular practice—say, fasting or vigils—we simply pay attention to how we react when someone injures or offends us. We observe the rising passions within us, we listen to the sudden hailstorm of angry thoughts, and we take note of how quickly and easily we are led to the brink of sin. The next time around, we are better armed against that automatic sense of self-righteous affront. Perhaps, in time, we can respond with patience rather than rage.

This is the reason the desert dwellers were famous for welcoming what we would consider to be disaster. They knew how to mine every hardship for its spiritual gold.

In more than one story from this era, for example, an elder is robbed of what little he retains. Instead of hunting down the thief and demanding back a precious prayer book or crucifix, the victimized elder invariably welcomes as a brother the person who has "lightened his burden" by stealing what had become overly important.

On a still deeper level, to counteract vainglory (the thirst for public approval) the abbas and ammas (spiritual fathers and mothers) were willing to accept blame and shame for what they hadn't done. In more than one case, an elder was falsely accused of fathering a child and humbly accepted responsibility for its care. When, years later, the truth was finally revealed, there were no recriminations. Through trudging faithfully down this hard and painful road, vainglory had been thwarted.

Desert wisdom about turning trouble to good use reappears in new form fourteen hundred years later in the writings of St. Thérèse of Lisieux. In *The Story of a Soul*, she describes her "little way," which is a practice of joyfully welcoming humiliation, frustrated desire, sorrow, and even intense physical suffering as the fastest route to spiritual growth and maturation. In her case, growing up quickly was especially important, for she died at twenty-four.

To contemporary readers, Thérèse's writings border on the scandalous. In an era that looks upon any kind of suffering as an abomination to be eradicated as soon as possible, whether through medical technology, drugs, psychological counseling, or social programs, the "little way" looks suspiciously like masochism, justified by a fanatical piety. For Thérèse, however, as for the wisdom of the desert, embracing the traumas of life as opportunities rather than tragedies was not about harboring self-hatred but instead about fostering love. More, they understood, as C.S. Lewis later understood, that we are still living in "enemy-occupied territory." Spiritual evil still roams the world, and it is much stronger than we are in our merely natural state. We need to become tougher. The mortifications that come our way through daily life help kill the self-centeredness that blocks grace and the help of the Holy Spirit.

watching the thoughts to prepare ourselves for forgiveness

One of the most profound insights offered by desert spirituality—one that was picked up by those who wrote early monastic "rules for life"—was the notion of "watching the thoughts" as a way to "guard the heart" against temptations toward self-elevating thinking and behavior. Indeed, modern cognitive therapists advise their clients to use a version of the same practice.

Evagrius Ponticus speaks about this method in his *Praktikos,* a manual on prayer and the spiritual life. He names and describes the "eight evil thoughts" that lead us quickly into sin: repetitive thoughts having to do with food, sex, and possessions (gluttony, lust, and avarice); sadness (about the things we long for but can't have); anger; spiritual boredom (called *acedia*); self-elevation (also known as vainglory); and pride. Once a thought of this kind has insistently presented itself to us, we have a choice. We can either embrace it—in which case we will soon find ourselves ensnared by it—or we can block it the moment we spot it.

Evagrius points out that thoughts like these are only the innocent-looking openers for long trains of attached, and increasingly compelling, reasons to sin. If we allow the first intriguing thought to enter and make itself at home in us, particularly if we begin to turn it around and look at it from different directions, liking what we see, we are doomed to cave in to the subtle permission it conveys.

The thought of food, for example, might begin, as it does with me sometimes, with a simple image—a second glass of wine after 10:00 p.m. when it's been a stressful day. I say to myself, I'm tired and wound up and I've been having trouble with insomnia lately. If I don't get a good night's sleep, I'm dead tomorrow— and it's a big day. If I continue to stare longingly at the empty goblet, the train keeps chugging by: in fact, there's that meeting at 2:00 p.m. . . . If I'm falling asleep at the table, I'll look like an idiot. I've got a responsibility here! I have to sleep. Maybe I could take a sleeping pill?

But what I really want, of course, is wine, for wine has proven itself a stalwart friend when it comes to the problem of sleeplessness. Besides, I don't believe in sleeping pills, I piously remind myself. They can be addictive! And they make me feel groggy the next day. I *really* should have some wine instead—it's healthier.

A one-time argument with the self over a second glass of wine is not much of a problem. But when the same thought pops up the next evening, and then the next, and when (invariably) it's not about the second glass but the fourth and fifth, we've become enslaved to the sin of gluttony. Wine now rules us; we no longer control our own behavior when it comes to drinking.

And, as the Desert Fathers and Mothers point out, this long road to ruin begins with a single, persistent, and enticing thought that, deep inside, we don't want to resist in the first place. By allowing it to float around in our consciousness, we open greater and greater parts of ourselves to its influence. In time, we've veered off in a whole new direction, a path on which it may be incredibly difficult to retrace our steps.

But how do we block a thought like this? After all, it seems like the more we try to stop thinking about something, the more persistently it buzzes around inside our heads. The Fathers and Mothers were on to this too, and so advised that we never try to fight these thoughts on our own but instead immediately call on the name of the Lord. One ancient prayer for help goes like this: O God, come to my assistance, O Lord, make haste to help me! Another, developed later, is the famous Jesus Prayer: Jesus Christ, Son of God, have mercy on me a sinner.

The point is that once again we are replacing one habit with another—in this case, a thought that is trying to become habitual with a prayer for help. In time, that response becomes automatic. Without having to think about it, we immediately begin the cry for help when we're under siege by an alluring thought.

In the collected writings of the spiritual masters of the Christian East known as the Philokalia, which includes a lot of desert wisdom, it is clear that the method of thought watching is key. And for more than a thousand years, Orthodox Christian monks on Mount Athos in Greece have continued to faithfully practice this mental discipline that once fostered such holiness in the original Christian desert dwellers. So do I.

guarding the heart from evil

The second part of the desert method for dealing with the temptation toward evil is called the "guarding of the heart." The term *heart,* as used by the Hebrews, refers to the personhood of the individual human being. It is the core of the self, the place of deepest emotional life where love abides. But it is even more than this: the heart is the center where all things meet.

Modern writers, such as the French monk André Louf, refer to the heart as the "organ of prayer," the communication link with the divine. As such, it is particularly vulnerable to spiritual invasion. The Desert Fathers and Mothers believed that we watch the thoughts in order to guard the heart from incursions by Satan and his agents.

The contemporary West has pretty much abandoned the ancient belief in spiritual evil. When we find ourselves baffled by the vicious brutality of a serial killer or the systematic slaughter of a people, as in Cambodia under Pol Pot, or more recently in Rwanda under the Hutus, we immediately seek a psychological explanation rather than a spiritual one: what terrible things happened to these people as children?

Yet no matter what we're able to unearth (for example, the psychological profile done by the U.S. government on Hitler before we went to war), we are still at a loss to explain the upwelling of such massive evil. We no longer understand, as our forebears did, the concept of evil as a personal spiritual being, one whose machinations lie at the root of any true horror. The psychologists of the desert, however, were also spiritual masters who not only believed in Satan and demonic beings, but regularly inter-acted with them.

For the desert—the place of desolation described in Isaiah, fit only for the screech owl, the great owl, and the raven—was the alleged dwelling place of the devil. To voluntarily spend one's life in the wilderness was to deliberately court satanic attack. The ascetic behavior of the desert dwellers was, to a large degree, about this element of their struggle. They believed their job was to develop, through prayer and ascesis, pure enough hearts to engage in spiritual warfare on behalf of the rest of the world.

Missionaries, priests, and nuns who nowadays live in non-Western parts of the world generally have a more nuanced view of spiritual evil than the rest of us, including those of us who are devout. They may have experienced witchcraft firsthand, or seen what happens to people when a sorcerer gets angry. They have likely been approached by parishioners with pleas for deliverance or even exorcism.

Yet we shudder at the thought. Two centuries of awe at the wonders of technology have done their work on the Western Christian mind. We have been taught since the Enlightenment that anything we can't prove in a laboratory or explain in otherwise scientific terms is nothing but primitive superstition. More, we're done with the devil, except as some kind of ludicrous cartoon figure. As writer Nicholas Delbanco points out in his book *The Death of Satan,* the devil immigrated from Europe with the first Puritan settlers but began to fade from American consciousness surprisingly early in our history. Why? For one thing, he was too strongly linked with the things we wanted to pursue. He was the embarrassing reminder of a moral outlook that got in the way of getting ahead.

Interestingly enough, however, a healthy respect for Satan and his wiles can actually make it *easier* to forgive than when we limit the scope of our thinking solely to the psychological. We are open to the notion that something more is at work than meets the eye, something that capitalizes on our emotional weaknesses and undisciplined wills. We can more easily understand why Jesus, who performed numerous exorcisms, kept talking about "releasing the captives." The person who acts under the impulse of demonic evil is, in a very real sense, enslaved.

The rigorous and austere life of the desert dweller was not simply evidence of his or her spiritual ambition, then, but a concerted attempt to change patterns of thinking and behaving so as to protect the spiritual core from this kind of invasion and enslavement. At stake was the integrity of the organ of prayer—the communication center from which one interacted with God.

With the heart intact, one could live under what is often called the "double command of love." As Christ says, "You shall love the Lord, your God, with all your heart, with all your soul, and with all your mind [and] . . . You shall love your neighbor as yourself" (Mt. 22:37, 39). Here lies the explanation for some of the more amazing stories about the desert elders and their seemingly endless ability to embrace the wicked and transform them into repentant believers—and sometimes even new monks.

Their expansive *caritas* (love), however, had little to do with the kind of universal tolerance preached today. What they saw in another human being, no matter how degraded, was a fellow soul made in the image and likeness of the God they adored. The greatest of these spiritual masters could not bear the thought that anyone, no matter what he or she had done, should be condemned by his or her own hardness of heart to live apart from God.

Under this view, forgiveness is as necessary and natural as rain (and as Christ reminds us, God causes his sun to rise on both the good and the evil, and his rain to fall on both the righteous and unrighteous). We hear the implicit message of forgiveness in Mother Teresa's injunction to "love the Christ in everyone." We had it modeled for us—and were baffled—after the shootings in the Amish schoolhouse at Nickel Mines.

To hold a grudge is to play the devil's game. The longer we shut up our heart against others, no matter what they have done to us, the closer we come to losing *caritas* entirely. Whether we harden our heart toward someone who has offended us or allow our heart to be invaded by the demons of wrath, envy, jealousy, avarice, or pride, the result is the same: our spiritual orientation enters into a slow rotation away from God. When the heart is naively left unguarded—when we think that nothing we experience, ponder, or feel can hurt us, for we are in charge of ourselves—then without even

knowing what is happening to us, we find that
the compass needle set by our innate, magnetic
attraction to good has shifted slightly, then
shifted again.

how continual prayer and forgiveness connect

Modern-day monks, the heirs to desert spirituality, are the first to admit that the friction
generated by living in close proximity can tempt
them into grudges between brother and brother
or sister and sister. What saves them from the
hell of settled animosity at close quarters? Father
Arthur, a former Franciscan and for many years
now a Camaldolese Benedictine, once told me,
"It's hard for anger to get obsessive when we're
praying with the person we're mad at four times
a day." Prayer in this circumstance becomes a
balm that soothes and can even extinguish the
burning heat of rage.

When longtime friends of ours recently broke
the news that they were getting a divorce and
nothing could stop them, the first thing I wanted
to say to them was this: pray for one another

daily. Whether or not this changes your decision to end your marriage and live separately, if you are faithful to the discipline of daily prayer for one another, you are far less likely to succumb to the myriad temptations that hover around divorce: the temptation toward vengeance, toward slander, toward using your children as a weapon. Your heart, broken though it may be, will be guarded through prayer.

When we constantly refer our life back to God, even in its smallest details, we give up the illusion that we are free and self-contained beings who can do what we like, including nursing and cherishing our anger, without affecting anyone else. This familiar mantra—as long as I'm not hurting anyone, it's nobody's business what I do—is not and can never be a Christian point of view. In his beautiful image of the vine and the branches, Christ presents a deep and sobering truth about our much-vaunted human freedom. Not only are we connected with one another on a fundamental level, we are intertwined with him. "Apart from me," he says, "you can do nothing" (Jn. 15:5).

Continual prayer keeps that truth before our eyes and helps protect us against the powerful temptation to try going it alone. And when we are constantly in touch with God, Satan cannot enter.

six false forgiveness

WHEN I WAS FIRST LIVING in that village in Honduras, I had not yet truly experienced the suffering of others firsthand. But I would never have been in Honduras at all if my parents hadn't taught me that it was good to be concerned about others. The lesson came at a price.

I remember being ten and sitting in front of the TV with my mother, watching the first march for civil rights take place in Selma, Alabama. Though I had been told about the situation in the South, it was not until I saw Bull Connor's police dogs lunging at little children, or high-intensity fire hoses aimed full force at peaceful marchers, that I had any inkling of what it all meant.

Overnight, I was transformed from a state of innocence to experience, as the poet William

Blake would put it. I could no longer cling to the childish notion that everyone was good and could be trusted, but this was a hard lesson to swallow; it gave me nightmares and ruined my sleep. The truth about evil roaming loose in the world felt like a crippling burden. And I felt responsible for doing something about it.

My teenaged experience of large-scale suffering in Honduras only added to the weight. And the attendant loss of faith darkened my worldview considerably. When, as an adult, I finally found the atheist existentialists, I thought I'd come home: These were people who saw what I saw. These were people who knew all about the ominous river that ran beneath the bright and shining surface of life. These were people who knew life was hopeless, but behaved with nobility despite their angst.

In the interim between my loss of faith and the discovery of these soul mates, however, I got a temporary but bracing lift from the music of John Lennon. According to him, everything was far easier than it looked. We simply had to give peace a chance. We simply had to make love, not war. We simply had to forget about heaven and hell, and focus instead at what lay before our eyes—the beauty of the animals, of trees and sky and sea. If we wanted it badly enough, we could simply laugh evil in the face and it would wither up and disappear like the Wicked Witch of the East.

For several years, this lovely fantasy served to mask the abyss that had opened up inside when I walked away from God. But living in fantasy is like living in quicksand—the deeper we sink, the more we scramble to shore things up, when, all the time, the only way out is to be rescued.

When fantasy is coupled with Christian belief, not only do we pervert our faith, but we wind up as prisoners of our own minds. Why? We have lost the truth. As members of various truth and reconciliation commissions have pointed out, unless we are willing to face reality, genuine forgiveness is not possible.

Shortly after I found myself being drawn back into Christianity, and while I was still trying to sort out the differences between true Christian hope and John Lennon's bright, shallow optimism, I became involved with a youth center in south central Los Angeles. In response to urban violence, our organization was invited to a weekend-long conference to improve race relations. The point, we were told, was to do some heavy-duty confronting in a controlled setting. This no-holds-barred approach was meant to cut through the usual syrupy platitudes and get at the core of the race problem in America. By the end of the conference, we were assured, we would have forgiven one another and become lifelong friends. But first we had to do *the work*.

During our first session, I scanned the room with hopeful optimism. Truly, this all seemed like such a good—even noble—idea, considering the level of repressed but explosive anger we'd witnessed during the recent Los Angeles riots. If we could only *connect,* then everything would work itself out. First, however, we had to get over our fear of one another.

I had to admit that I was secretly becoming nervous. In one corner lounged five gang members, their necks ringed by tattoos. In another sat six stolid ex-cons, pointedly garbed in blue denim. Directly across from me, somebody who turned out to be a Central American gunrunner sat glaring at several women whose dark green T-shirts announced that they were "Proud to Be Lesbian Tradeswomen." Groups kept pouring into the room, including a bewildered antinuclear organization from Utah who seemed to have signed up for the wrong conference. People bristled and flexed and cast threatening looks at one another.

Our conference leaders, who didn't look older than twenty, began by dividing us up into "cohorts" for a lengthy let-it-all-hang-out session about how we *really* felt about "the other." We were placed in our groups on the basis of ethnicity, gender, and sexual orientation. And we were strongly encouraged to "speak out"—to say anything and everything that came to mind. The only rule was absolute loyalty to the cohort; we were not to communicate what was said to anybody else. We'd have our chance to do that later, when group was intentionally pitted against group.

There were five people in my cohort, three of them from the still-baffled antinuclear organization. One of these began to wail as she tried to describe the damage she had suffered through being labeled an irredeemable racist, simply by virtue of her skin color. "It's not fair!" she kept moaning. "I can't help it if I'm white. I've been victimized for political purposes! I'm completely *blind* to race."

Regardless of how accurate her assessment was, I could see that her anguish was real. And nothing we were told to do the rest of the weekend helped heal such anguish, which seemed to be endemic among our group of retreatants. It was the failure of this group, of that experience, that led me to see something important about when forgiveness is possible. We were facing something very big here, and those old idealisms of mine were completely ineffectual in such a setting.

In the long run, the retreat only served to confirm what a formidable power social hatred can be. Our workshop leaders, not surprisingly, ended the two-day session by declaring they would never hold another conference in Los Angeles.

Despite the best intentions of the sociologists who designed this event, we did not wind up as lifelong friends, or even civil acquaintances. All that honest "sharing" was wasted. We listened, we felt accused, we got defensive, we blew up at each other. When all was said and done, we were (sadly enough) the same ragtag collection of unenlightened sinners we'd been before we came to Malibu. Why did it fail?

The goal of the conference, never fully articulated in these terms, was mutual forgiveness. Why was it impossible under these circumstances? Was it simply the overwhelming diversity of the group that did it? Was it nothing more than our inability to communicate what it was like to be uniquely *us?* No, the conference was doomed because it was structured around a false premise, which was that simply expressing our feelings would heal them. This well-intentioned enterprise failed because it took a naïve and simplistic stance to wrongdoing; though presenting itself as a hard-hitting exercise in truth-telling, it was at bottom designed to prove John Lennon's thesis that "all we need is love."

Love, however, is effectively blocked by chronic rage, murderous resentment, habitual distrust, smoldering envy, self-protective anxiety, and institutionalized animosity. In order to love, those weapons must be first laid down. Nobody in the workshop showed us how to do that, or even told us we should. Real forgiveness, however, starts there—at the moment we decide to give up the arsenal and open ourselves to the possibility of repentance, confession, and absolution.

This ill-fated attempt to improve race relations in Los Angeles was foiled by a form of sentimentality that is insidious in our culture today. A deep-rooted naïvety about the reality of sin and evil still lingers on in my generation, which was formed by young geniuses like John Lennon, and by music that addressed our unspoken yearning to be rid of the burden of darkness we had inherited from our parents—wounded survivors of the Depression and a horrifying World War.

Many of us sixties kids embraced a sentimental view of reality. The religious version of this crippling sentimentality encourages several different kinds of pseudoforgiveness. In the first, we try our best to forgive because doing so makes us "feel good about ourselves" rather than because we are trying to follow Christ. In the second, we forgive because "doing our duty" elevates us in our own eyes. In the third, we mistake Christ's injunction not to make hypocritical judgments with a call for universal religious and moral tolerance that denies the reality of evil altogether. In all three cases, the point of Christ's injunction to forgive—"love one another as I have loved you"—has been distorted or lost entirely.

sentimental faith

The nineteenth-century Danish philosopher Søren Kierkegaard devoted a good bit of his intellectual attention to the problem of what was going wrong with the church of his day. As he points out in his hard-hitting critique called *Training in Christianity*, people in his time seemed to be more interested in satisfying the demands of bourgeois convention than in becoming disciples of Christ—in other words, more interested in how they appeared to others than in how they really were. The Christian moral life, he believed, was in danger of being disconnected from its source.

In another work, *Either/Or,* he describes a different kind of disconnection, the severing of an emotional response from the object that inspires it. Emotions are evidence that we care about something, that it has value for us. The first time we really fall in love, for example, we are flooded with a cataract of emotion so overwhelming that we can't even eat or sleep for a while. We feel joy and terror and longing and baffled disbelief, all at the same time. We are an emotional mess—all because the beloved has overnight become the very center of our life.

When the emotional response rather than the actual, living person becomes the real point, however, we've become a sentimentalist, someone who revels in the high that accompanies intense feeling. Instead of offering ourselves to the object of our devotion in concrete, loving ways, we sit alone atop an emotional treasure pile, gloating over our own euphoria and working on ways to retrigger it when it begins to cool.

Kierkegaard uses the term *aesthete* to describe this kind of emotional junkie—someone who spends his or her life restlessly seeking out experiences that will provide a high. When we are religious aesthetes, we can delight in the hushed beauty of a church, the glow of candlelight on icons, the clouds of rising incense, the music of Scripture being read aloud, but we look upon worship as primarily an *artistic* rather than a *spiritual* experience. Church is valuable to us because it "moves" us. We admire it from afar, without a modicum of personal commitment, and we are thus very likely to move on to something more interesting when the whole thing becomes old hat. As aesthetes, we want "to have the effect without the cause." And as aesthetes, we choose to forgive primarily because it makes *us* feel good.

I believe that my years as a secular activist were often characterized by this kind of sentimental complacency. I admired myself for being properly outraged over issues like race and war and poverty and political oppression. I enjoyed the high of being "all steamed up" over the evils of society. However, this passion of mine rarely led me to make real sacrifices, and in fact (as it was so vehemently pointed out to me at the conference on race relations) I continued to reap all the benefits of the unjust system I was purportedly fighting.

True forgiveness, on the other hand, often requires an excruciating level of self-sacrifice. A person who forgives for sentimental reasons may actually be seeking relief from pain instead of real reconciliation. He wants to feel good, no matter what, and he's willing to shove deeply troubling, incontrovertible facts aside to get there. Underneath, sad to say, often lies a cold and selfish heart.

More admirable by far, according to Kierkegaard, is the ethical person who acts on principle, regardless of the emotional effect this generates. He or she looks for guidance to a broad and noble set of rules for life, and is (unlike the uncommitted aesthete) consistent and self-disciplined. However, for the Christian person of duty, the temptation can be toward legalism: like the Pharisees Jesus so sternly chastises, we strictly uphold the law for its own sake, rather than because morality is meant to make us better people, foster love in us, and help us handle spiritual power. Thus, when Jesus tells us we must forgive, we dutifully scramble to comply.

Fervently and sincerely, we try our best to forgive. And we may even convince ourselves that we have successfully met the challenge; we have bravely set aside our own emotions and our distaste for those who flout the moral law, in order to comply. But something isn't right. Everything in us cries out for hard-hitting justice, not forgiveness. We have to swallow and swallow our hidden contempt for the people who have sinned against us. And we are tempted to compensate for this terrible unease by assuring ourselves of our own moral superiority. We tell ourselves that (unlike the common run of folks) we have been "big" enough to do what Christian duty requires.

As C.S. Lewis reminds us, all other sins are as mere fleabites in comparison to pride. And the pridefulness of believing ourselves morally superior and acting toward others on the basis of that self-identity is the antithesis of God's merciful loving-kindness. If our attempts to forgive are not born out of our love for Christ and our deep desire to give him what he has asked for, no matter how difficult or impossible sounding, they are doomed.

When we are pious people of duty, our pseudoforgiveness can be worse for others than our settled enmity, for the recipients of our supposed largesse can never feel truly at peace. Instead, they are condemned to wondering: Has she *really* let this go? Can we truly be friends again? Is he just tolerating me because the Bible says he has to?

you can't forgive without relating

True forgiveness, according to Christ, is inextricably linked to *relationships*. Loving relationships are precious and built over a period of years. At times they suffer grievous setbacks. They only mature when the people who are in them grow up spiritually, which means they become more virtuous, wiser, and more loving.

Sadly, the contemporary American cosmic lovers, like I was in the sixties, are often not very serious about their new religion, but are simply people who have rejected the church of their childhood and substituted in its place a hodgepodge of beliefs they find personally pleasing. Their solution to the trauma of the world is often a simplistic one, and totally incapable of dealing with the gravity of evil. Their attitude toward forgiveness is much like Rodney King's—"Can't we all just get along?" Forgiveness in this sense has very little to do with sin, confession, and reconciliation, but is instead a thinly veiled synonym for radical tolerance. If we never condemn what is wrong or try to point out the difference between truth and falsity, nobody gets upset.

As I look back on that ill-fated conference on race relations, I can see that the impetus was a good one. Somebody had worked very hard at trying to heal the gaping wound that had so dramatically manifested itself during the urban riots. But true forgiveness requires grace, in addition to the virtue of supernatural caritas. And when good works are conducted in a vacuum—outside the sphere of God's loving reign—while they may temporarily lead to improvement, they are inevitably doomed to failure, for they are not rooted in the one foundation that can nourish and sustain them.

part 3
forgiving

*radical love for those
who have hurt us*

seven forgiving those we do not choose (parents)

I AM ONE OF THE LUCKY ONES. I came from a family that loved each other. And my parents were both good people who tried their best to teach us how to be decent human beings. More, they raised us in the church, and because of them, I had a religious background that helped me see what was lacking when, many years later, I realized I could no longer handle myself on my own.

At my dad's funeral fifteen years ago, one of the most poignant eulogies we heard came from a longtime business acquaintance, a man my father often had to visit in his role as company credit manager. Though chances were good that most of their conversations over the years had to do with money and why this customer needed to pay up on his account in a more expeditious manner, what he said to our family was this: "Your father was one of the finest gentlemen I've ever met."

We knew what he meant. Our father always treated us—my mother and his five children—with the utmost warmth and affectionate courtesy. Even when we were kids, he respected us as people. But we were not the only recipients of his quiet, beaming love. Everyone who met him was drawn to his gentleness and twinkling good will. He had the gift of joy in life, and in our eyes, he was a kind of saint. Thus, none of us were surprised at this choked-up tribute from a former customer.

My mother showed her love in a different way. From the time we were infants, she was our teacher. One of my favorite old family photos is of me, at two, dressed in a mini-version of my mother's beautiful blue dress and standing on a sofa cushion beside her, both of us playing our flutes. Hers was the real deal, elegant and silver, and she played it extremely well and still can.

Mine was toddler-sized, but in my mind, she and I were playing music *together*.

What my mom gave all of us was a sense of our own uniqueness as people. From the time we were born, she knew us in an intimate and personal way, and thus she could help guide us into our adult vocations. I suspect she'd already discerned on the day that photo was taken, for example, that the life of a flautist was not for me. Instead, she read to me for hours, instilling in me a love for words that eventually flowered into a call. I'm a writer primarily because of her.

With such a family background, it would seem I had little or no reason to need to forgive my parents. All was good. Yet forgiving them took me many years.

Why? What had they done that was so hurtful? The answer is easy: with all their efforts, they had not managed to produce a perfect person—and I found ways to resent that. Like every young adult launching herself into a challenging world, I had undeveloped places in me, blind spots and immaturities, fears and misconceptions. I was unprepared for things my parents never thought I'd face, and I suffered woefully because of this. I was also headstrong and determined to be independent at a very young age, and so I took on adult life with only half the tools I needed. I found myself raising kids of my own without yet having grown up myself. I struggled and failed in my first marriage, and I made decisions that kept me from finishing college for years. When I looked angrily around for a reason, the obvious one was staring me in the face: They Had Failed Me.

The natural tendency to blame our parents for everything we don't like about ourselves may be more pronounced in my generation, I suspect, than in any that have lived before. One reason for this extra measure of generational hostility on our part comes straight out of the political turmoil of the sixties, when we learned to "question authority" and scorn those who complied with the draft. To our parents, who had enlisted for the duty in the battlefields of Europe and the Pacific, and who had sacrificed their boyfriends, husbands, and brothers by the tens of thousands to a different war, our attitude must have seemed incredibly naïve and childish. The gap in perception was almost unbridgeable—and we felt and resented the weight of their disapproval during what *we* considered to be our finest hour.

Thanks to psychology, we found another reason to blame our parents. Psychoanalytic theory in particular focuses on the child/parent relationship as the root of most adult problems. Though Freud also influenced our parents' generation, they were not financially or culturally disposed to undergo analysis or any other kind of psychotherapy. We, on the other hand, turned to psychology in droves, perhaps as a substitute for organized religion. Psychology became our particular pathway to self-understanding, and that path inevitably led back to the people who raised us.

Finally, I think we blamed our parents for the burdens they carried from their Depression-era childhoods and their wartime sufferings—burdens we could neither imagine nor share, but that in some ways darkened our lives too. Our parents were generally a taciturn group, having been raised to keep their troubles to themselves, and so it usually did not occur to them that we might need to hear their stories— not just out of curiosity, but to understand some of what they experienced and how those experiences had sifted down to us.

Despite this very real generation gap, I am nowadays filled with fond gratitude for the way I was brought up. Some of this has come from raising children myself and finding out just what sacrifices are involved and how many mistakes a person can make. Some of it has been inspired by the continued closeness and friendship among my siblings. But then again, I am one of the lucky ones. Others are not so fortunate. What about those whose parents are brutal or cruel or simply absent? What about people whose parents are alcoholic, drug-addicted, or seriously mentally ill? What about those who have never known that their mother or father loved them? The damage that results from such relationships can be crippling, and forgiveness can understandably seem like a complete impossibility.

catastrophic damage

When we were in elementary school, my friend Nathan always wore long pants to hide the black and blue bruises on his legs. When he got to be a teenager, he started keeping a baseball bat under the bed. And then, one day, he realized he'd grown large enough to fight back. His father never tried to beat him up again, but the damage was done: Nathan left and never went back.

But he had to live for years with an internal battle raging inside between the person—and especially the *father*—he wanted to be for his own son's sake, and the demon he knew could take him over at the slightest provocation. After years of silent, painful struggle, made bearable primarily by the love of a strong and tender wife, he realized he'd finally conquered the specter of explosive violence that had for so long threatened to destroy his own family.

It was only then, he told me, that he was able to consider forgiveness. Though it took a long time to calm the emotions that boiled up whenever he deliberately thought of the father he'd fled so long ago, he stayed with it. And finally, one day, he got in the car and drove hundreds of miles to see him. When he walked to the door and rang the bell, the old man who opened it didn't recognize his son. But Nathan said what he'd come to say: "I forgive you." His father cried and apologized for the inexplicable cruelty that had nearly destroyed a helpless child.

When I asked Nathan if he now wanted to pursue the relationship, he smiled and shook his head. "Once was enough," he told me. "I just needed to see him one time, and let him see me, before he died. I needed to let him know he was forgiven. But I don't feel any compulsion to draw him into my life. He doesn't need to be a part of my son's world."

Nathan's story is an example of true forgiveness. He laid down his entirely justifiable anger in order to offer his onetime oppressor the gift of forgiveness in person. But there was no attempt at reconciliation, in the sense of attempting to develop a new relationship. Why? For one thing, Nathan couldn't be sure his father wouldn't try to hurt him again, psychologically rather than physically this time, and he wasn't about to risk being swept once more into the long corridors of anger. He especially wasn't willing to risk that for his son.

Genuine forgiveness, in other words, does not necessarily require reconciliation. Prudence might require that we keep a safe distance from those who are not yet healed of their propensity to wreak havoc in other lives. In many cases, when we manage to lay down our justifiable anger over the witting or unwitting brutality of a parent, and to wish that person well, we have done enough. By refusing to be drawn into the cycle of evil, we've effectively broken the generational curse.

The psychiatrist Barry Grosskopf writes movingly of the way that the fourth commandment, "Honor your father and your mother, that you may have a long life in the land which the Lord, your God, is giving you" (Ex. 20:12), changed the way he dealt with many of his clients. He realized that he couldn't really help people come to terms with their childhoods separate from this basic truth: they couldn't change the fact that their parents were their parents. And somehow they had to learn to honor the people who'd given birth to them, regardless of how miserably they may have failed in their parental roles.

Consequently, he began teaching his clients to imagine their mothers and fathers as children— the historical era they lived through, the financial circumstances of the time, their own parents. And in the process, he discovered the link between the fourth commandment and the first, which says that the fathers' sins shall cause suffering to the third and fourth generations of those that follow.

Though I believe it is true that my generation learned to use our parents as a comprehensive excuse for our own failings, this is not to say that any of us remain unaffected by our parents' choices. Sometime we must deal with the long-term results of their almost forgotten sins. Sometimes we must cope with their settled disappointment over a botched life. And sometimes we ourselves must bear the weight of their unhealed grief.

Grosskopf realized that in his own early years, he had been quietly handed the burden of his mother and father's World War II childhood trauma. Jews faced with the prospect of the death camps, they'd fled to Russia where they'd nearly starved. Their experience was so overwhelmingly bad that as adults with their own family, they'd resolved never to speak of it. Grosskopf says that though the household was a loving one, it was almost visibly haunted by this silent grief and pain. But since nobody ever explained what was going on, he simply absorbed this mysterious heaviness and carried it on with him into his own adult life, where for some years it crippled him.

the vulnerability of the child

Not only do our parents pass their own burdens on to us, they bequeath us what they received from *their* mothers and fathers, backward into the mists of our ancestral beginnings. Regardless of whether or not Freud's theories about the human psyche are accurate descriptions of our nature (the Christian view is quite different), he was certainly on to something when he pointed toward childhood as the seedbed of adult life. When we are still immature and inexperienced children, we cannot possibly grasp the full meaning of what we are wordlessly experiencing. Instead, this emotional mystery becomes part of our landscape, the psychological home in which we must forever after live.

For example, when my grandmother was two, her mother died, and even though she was sixty-nine and I was only eighteen when I heard this story for the first time, I somehow recognized the shell-shocked mental landscape she was describing. We sat facing one another on separate twin beds in what used to be the guestroom of the old farmhouse but now served as her widow's quarters. I was there to keep her company after my grandfather's funeral.

On the dresser was a sepia photograph in a metal frame: her father's wedding picture, taken in 1888, in front of the just-built clapboard house with its hand-carved Norwegian gingerbread. Her father, lean and serious and looking older than his years, sported an impressive handlebar mustache. Her mother was a dark-eyed beauty with masses of Gibson-girl hair and a waist her husband could no doubt span with his hands.

Grandma picked up the framed picture and handed it to me, and while I studied it in the lamplight, she talked. For a while after her mother's death, she said, she was too young to comprehend what it all meant, just that she was lonely and frightened and couldn't sleep. Her older sisters tried their best to fill the gap, but it was a dark and painful time for her. She felt as though she were constantly crying, even when there were no tears.

Thus, a few years later when her dad came home with a young woman on his arm, she was tremendously excited, especially when the children were told that this pretty lady was going to be their new stepmother. When her father and his bride got back from their brief honeymoon and the household had settled down, she shyly approached the stranger who had come to live with them, trying out a word she hadn't used since toddlerhood: *Mother.*

"And she *hit* me," Grandma said in fresh wonderment, tears springing to her eyes. "She slapped my cheek and said, 'Don't you *ever* call me that again. I'm not your mother. Your mother is *dead*.'"

More than six decades had come and gone since that moment of unthinking cruelty. At some point, Grandma learned to live with and even love her stepmother, and in fact watched over her when she was old and frail. But the experience of that rejecting slap, so unexpected and undeserved, was as immediate, I could see, as the day it happened. It had been burned into her, a bright scar that would never fade. It was part of who she was, and she would carry it, an unwanted lump of grief and bewilderment, in her heart until she died.

This, and far worse, is what parents can do to us. The effect is exponentially increased because of the natural idolatry that comes with total dependence. In our childhood years, our parents are everything to us. Betrayal cannot be borne—not without major collateral damage. During such a vulnerable stage, even an offhand remark at the right moment from one whom we adore can open a wound that never quite closes. For we see ourselves through their eyes. They are our gods.

Regarding the tender souls of children, Jesus says in a passage that can be read as referring either to young human beings or to "baby" Christians, "Things that cause people to sin will inevitably occur, but woe to the person through whom they occur. It would be better for him if a millstone were put around his neck and he be thrown into the sea than for him to cause one of these little ones to sin" (Lk. 17:1–3). The roots of our adult sin patterns are often to be found in the still-gaping wounds of childhood. Though some of us may have only minor hurts to get past and others may be traumatized in brutal ways, no one can escape that particular cause and effect. We are all faced with the necessity of forgiving our parents for the inadvertent or intentional harm they have caused us. But how?

Grosskopf's findings suggest that we first use our imaginations to divest our mothers and fathers of their aura of infallibility. In their authoritarian guise, they appear invincible, and their words ring so loudly down the ages that they can determine the way we see ourselves as human beings. Yet their infallibility precludes our mercy. If they are infallible, they have no excuse for hurting us. My husband, for example, shadow-boxed with his larger-than-life father for years, and could not allow himself to see the weaknesses in his dad until he himself was in his fifties. Only after he toppled the idol could he begin to relate to him as a person instead of a demanding mentor.

The next step in forgiving our parents is to try to see them as vulnerable children themselves, powerless to change their own family circum-stances. My dad, for instance, was ten years old in 1933, at the height of the Great Depression. My grandparents lost their farm and had to rent land from somebody else until they were finally able to buy their place back from the bank. Though he never talked much about those frightening times, they were stamped into his personality. I picked up on this trait in him very early on in the form of nightmares that had to do with facing evil alone and unprotected.

The third step in forgiving our parents is trying our best to understand how family history shaped the adults they became. After the financial catastrophe that to a large degree defined his childhood, my father was understandably worried about being able to support his own children. He bore tremendous work-related stress for years rather than take the chance of losing his job. At forty-nine, he had a near-fatal heart attack. And he died only a year or so after a retirement he postponed longer than he should have. Ironically, his early death may have caused the family more grief and suffering than we'd have gone through if he'd risked his job to spare himself at least some of that killing stress.

The fourth step in parental forgiveness is determining how this emotional inheritance has manifested itself in our own lives. Though my siblings will no doubt disagree with me, I can still see traces of my parents' Depression-generated childhood anxiety in all of us. Some of us work too hard, others worry too much, and several of us (including me) grapple with our dad's perennial insomnia. And these traits are already showing up in the generation below us, our young adult sons and daughters struggling to make a go of it in an increasingly competitive society. Just as our parents did, we have passed our anxieties on to our children.

The fifth aspect of parental forgiveness has to do with letting go of anger. Even though I can accept the reasons for my parents' anxiety, I've also had to live with that anxious hum in my own head since very early on. It has skewed many of my decisions and affected my relationships. For a while I was especially vulnerable to jealousy, for example. If someone I loved seemed to prefer another to me, my whole security seemed to be at stake, and I grew fiercely self-defensive. When I realized how this was connected to my parent's anxiety, I got mad—mad at the way this inherited trait had bent my life, and mad because it had driven me to hurt people. And I wanted to blame *them* for that. Yet I couldn't lay down my own anxiety until I first dropped my anger and owned up to my personal responsibility in the matter.

forgiving what can't be helped

My friend Leslie Leyland Fields has written powerfully about her nonrelationship with her father. She and her siblings grew up believing that not only did he not love them, he was not remotely interested in the fact of their existence. As an adult, she married and moved to Alaska, where she had six children. One day she decided they should all make the journey to Florida to see the grandfather they'd never met. Despite the great sacrifice of time and family money this trip represented, she had few real expectations that the visit would change anything, and the modest hopes she did have were quickly dashed. Her father was still the same remote and emotionless man of her childhood, and appeared to take as little interest in his grandchildren as he once had in her. But now she was seeing him through different eyes—not the eyes of a wounded young girl, but the eyes of experienced adulthood. And she realized that she was looking not at a woefully inadequate, even hateful, parent, but at someone who was very likely seriously mentally ill.

She went home and researched her father's character traits until she was satisfied that she had found the answer. Though she could not confirm the diagnosis by getting him to a psychiatrist for evaluation, it seemed more than likely that he was suffering from a rare but severe personality disorder, one that meant he could not be in relationship with other people—one that meant he could not love. His world of concern was strictly limited to physical objects he could control—an afternoon ice cream cone, a favorite sailing magazine. No matter how beautiful her children were, and no matter how much she tried to get through to him, he was incapable of being moved.

When she realized how many years had been lost when there might, all along, have been a cure, she felt like weeping. But then she read further, finding at last the answer with which she had to live: there *was* no cure. What was and is shall ever be.

The realization that in some cases there are indeed uncrossable barriers to fuller, richer, healthier relationships can open our hearts to forgiveness in a way that great expectations, continually thwarted, cannot. Forgiveness may require that we give up our wistful, soul-deep, unrequited longing for more from the parents who may have given us life but are, for whatever reason, incapable of giving us love.

eight forgiving those we do choose (marriage partners)

ONE DAY WHILE I WAS STILL TEACHING, I got a real shock. I arrived at class, prepared to lecture on Leo Tolstoy's brilliant novella, *The Death of Ivan Ilyitch,* which my students were *supposed* to have read the night before. Knowing the troops, though, and realizing we were heading for the weekend, my expectations were appropriately low. I was tempted to give them a pop quiz, just to teach them that I really meant it when I gave them a reading assignment, but decided at the last minute that I didn't want to spend *my* hard-earned weekend doing school-work either.

I started the discussion by asking if anyone had a reaction to the novella that he or she would like to share. A young man promptly raised his hand and said that after reading what Tolstoy had to say about the futility of giving your life over to mindless work, he had been convinced of his own next step.

"Which is?" I asked, thinking this was all a joke.

"Which is that I'm dropping out of college. As of today." Then he turned around, nodded curtly at the class, and strode out the door. And I never did see him again.

Tolstoy is famous for having this kind of dramatic effect on his readers. For years a tortured agnostic, he wrote openly about his long struggle with Christian faith. When at age fifty-one he finally surrendered to God, his life was transformed, despite the fact he could never force himself to return to the Russian Orthodox Church. Alone, he did his utmost to come to terms with what he saw as the clear implications of the Sermon on the Mount, eventually adopting practices that baffled and offended both his family and his social circle. Tolstoy begins his preconversion masterpiece *Anna Karenina* with this sentence: "All happy families are alike, but an unhappy family is unhappy after its own fashion." The novel, which recounts the long, painful unraveling of a marriage, was inspired by a suicide he'd read about in the paper. One of the novel's most haunting qualities is the sense that nothing, including the terrible final scene, could have been avoided once the initial decision had been made. But Tolstoy includes a startling moment in the exact center of the book, one that, had the characters involved realized what was happening, had the power to turn the whole sad tale of adultery and unbearable sorrow into a symbol of the resurrection.

Anna, who has already left her bureaucrat husband Karenin for the dashing Count Vronsky, has just given birth to a daughter and appears to be dying of childbed fever. She orders a telegram sent to her estranged husband, begging him to come so that she can see him one last time. Though he is cynically convinced he's being made the victim of a self-serving trick, and though he is secretly hoping she *will* die and so rid him of the necessity of divorcing her, Karenin decides he must go. When he arrives, however, the first person he sees is Vronsky—the man who has destroyed his marriage and his reputation—sitting miserably huddled by the bed.

Karenin hesitates at the door, but the delirious Anna catches sight of him and draws him to her side where she gazes upon him with "tender and ecstatic affection" and tells him that now she understands it all. She begs him to forgive her. Amazed at her seemingly heartfelt repentance, Karenin feels his self-pitying anger begin to melt in the face of something larger than both of them.

Tolstoy writes, "He was not thinking that the Christian law which he had been trying to follow all his life enjoined on him to forgive and love his enemies; yet a glad feeling of love and forgiveness for his enemies filled his heart. He knelt down and laying his head in the curve of her arm, which burned like fire through her sleeve, he sobbed like a child."

Anna, however, who is desperate to heal the terrible situation she was responsible for creating, is not yet done. She now draws her lover forward, telling Karenin to pull Vronsky's hands away from his hidden face so that the two men can look into one another's eyes. Karenin obeys her, and uncovers in the other something "terrible with its look of agony and shame."

"Give him your hand. Forgive him," Anna commands.

And Karenin, the betrayed husband, extends the hand of forgiveness, "not attempting to restrain the tears that stream down his cheeks."

The exaltation Karenin feels at this moment is genuine, though his faith is so weak he cannot hang on to the infusion of grace that has briefly allowed him to transcend his angry sense of betrayal. Soon enough, he falls back into his calculating, self-protective ways, as do the momentarily repentant Anna and Vronsky when they realize she is not going to die after all. The intimacy of marriage amplifies the effects of sin, and Tolstoy seems to be making the point that forgiveness between marital partners must be ongoing if it is to be truly efficacious.

marriage as a leap of faith

When I went through a divorce over twenty-five years ago, a decision that came after thirteen years of marriage to a good man, I had a list of justifying reasons longer than my arm. The most important thing to me at the time was to do what I wanted to do—be with somebody else— but also to avoid shame at all costs. So it wasn't enough to be able to articulate all the sad but true facts about our "irreconcilable differences." I also needed to turn my failure at marriage into a noble act of heroism.

I *had* to leave, I told myself and anybody else who would listen. I'd gotten married so young, after all—only nineteen years old: a teenager!— and I'd never had the chance to "find myself." I'd taken on the full load of adult responsibility when I should have been going to college and learning who I was. Instead, I'd been consigned to boring clerical work in cramped offices. My spirit longed to spread its wings and soar. Being "tied down," even to a fine human being, not to mention two small children, was "killing my soul."

The important thing was that this divorce was "nobody's fault." It was "just the way things were." People "grow past" one another, I told myself, but there was no reason we "couldn't be friends" when it was all over.

The more I repeated this sad analysis of events, the more I found myself wallowing in sentimentality for what obviously "had to be." The hardheaded decision to move out so I could pursue another relationship got smothered somewhere beneath the billowing heaps of sentimental prose. It was as though I'd never made a decision at all, but had simply been swept up by cruel fate and now just had to make the best of it.

For many years, my refusal to face the truth because it would mean facing my own shame kept me from apologizing to my ex-husband for ruining our marriage. I could not even begin to look at the facts until after I'd returned to Christianity. There, in the heart of the church, I could no longer go on telling myself the self-deceiving lie. Ninety-eight percent of what happened to our partnership had to be laid at my door.

Though I told him I was sorry and sincerely begged his forgiveness, I could not yet bring myself to empathetically imagine what my betrayal had cost him in terms of emotional suffering. I could not bear to look at that, because I could not bear to imagine *myself* in that position. I was happily remarried, to Mike, by then, and the thought of being betrayed in the way I'd betrayed my first husband's trust was not to be borne. Whenever I mentally veered close to the subject, I got hammered by a terrible thought: if I could do that to *him,* anybody could do anything to anyone.

Despite my cowardice, that long-overdue conversation ended on a note I could not have anticipated—really, an unexpected manifestation of Christ's loving mercy. My ex-husband, who up until the moment I put the first crack in our marriage had been my one and only from the time I was fifteen, the loyal boyfriend whose letters had saved me from dying of homesickness in Honduras, said very gently, "But don't you know I forgave you years ago?"

I learned a lesson during that surprising moment that I have never forgotten. Committing our heart to another does indeed make us terribly vulnerable to suffering. My ex-husband had committed his heart to me and been grievously wounded in the process. But despite the great danger of giving ourselves away in love, this is our Christian vocation. As St. John so eloquently puts it, "Beloved, let us love one another, because love is of God; everyone who loves is begotten by God and knows God" (1 Jn. 4:7). These words ring particularly true in a marriage.

the marriages that make it

Though my marriage did not survive, others do. In the years since my divorce, I've met couples with far worse problems than we had who pulled themselves away from the brink. Usually, they emerge with a more realistic view of life, one that includes a quiet sorrow for the wounds they've inflicted on one another that may scar over in time but can never be fully eliminated. They no longer seem reckless or insouciant, and they've long since given up the fantasy of invincibility. For they've been broken in a way that precludes their ever returning to the foolish (and often self-centered) idealism of youth.

But along with sin-engendered regret and a permanent sense of compunction comes deep and joyful gratitude. By the mercy of God, they have been spared going through an amputation: the permanent severing of two lives that have grown, despite all differences, into a tangled mass of interconnected roots. If they have children, their gratitude is all the greater. Together, they can celebrate the great milestones of their kids' high school and college graduations, weddings, pregnancies, and new babies. Together, they can become grandparents, grow old, and help each other face death.

Even beyond thankfulness for the preservation of the family, however, comes gratitude for a new chance at intimacy and partnership. What has struck me about the couples who set out to save their marriages despite extreme circumstances like alcoholism, adultery, or financial ruin is the shy bloom of unexpected tenderness and love you can see on their faces. Someone they once believed they knew better than they knew themselves has turned into a complex and surprising stranger. They are intrigued and attracted; their hearts, once implacably hardened against one another, open like the lilies of Easter.

they forgive each other

Though there are fine programs available to couples in trouble, and though marriage counselors abound, couples who have managed to avoid divorce invariably point to forgiveness as the one thing necessary to marital survival. Without it, no amount of communication skills training, practice "dating," or talk therapy can avert disaster.

Unfortunately, however, when many marriages begin to break apart, there's a third party already waiting in the wings. An alluring new future beckons. One of the partners is so distracted by the fantasy of what life could be like that forgiving is the last thing on his or her mind.

Forgiving—genuinely forgiving—would mean letting go of all stored-up justifications for ending the marriage. The conflict of interest is too strong at this point to consider the one step that might prevent divorce.

Jesus knows exactly what goes on in such situations, and this is why he forbids divorce. He says to the Pharisees who ask him whether it is lawful to end a marriage, "What God has joined together, no human being must separate" (Mt. 19:6). When they question him about Mosaic law on the subject, he replies, "Because of the hardness of your hearts Moses allowed you to divorce your wives, but from the beginning it was not so. I say to you, whoever divorces his wife (unless the marriage is unlawful) and marries another commits adultery" (Mt. 19:8–9).

These words are shocking to the Pharisees, upstanding men of the church who assume they can make reasonable decisions about their own domestic lives. And they shock us even more today, we who are so committed to the notion of privacy and our inalienable right to pursue personal happiness. Given the unbending nature of Christ's injunction, it's easy to become self-defensive and thus overlook the key to understanding his position. When he speaks of "hardness of heart," he is speaking about more than two marriage partners withdrawing from one another. Hardness of heart always refers back to our relationship with God.

In other words, refusal to go as far as we possibly can to save a marriage is in a very real way a refusal to remain open to what God has in store for us within the circumstances of our lives *as they already exist.* The third-party distraction blinds us to this reality. Absorbed in our longing for something more personally fulfilling, we become deaf to God's voice and blind to his actions.

If nothing intervenes, we eventually lose God altogether. Though I did not make the connection for many years, it was not my eye-opening experience of suffering in Honduras that finally killed my relationship with God, but instead my extramarital love affair. The two could not coexist. By deliberately choosing to go my own way, I was in effect turning my face away from God. As Jesus reminds us, "No one can serve two masters. He will either hate one and love the other, or be devoted to one and despise the other" (Mt. 6:24).

If, on the other hand, we can set aside our fantasies about a different kind of future and hold our hearts open to the possibility of reconciliation, God can and does work miracles. The first step toward a marital miracle, however, has to be forgiveness. For example, we may have to set aside our perfectly justifiable anger and sense of betrayal in order to help free our partner from emotional bondage to someone else. On the other hand, we may have to set aside the list of old grievances that initially prompted our *own* straying before we can finally begin to "re-see" our spouse. If we can make these first forgiving steps toward one another, we make steps toward God. We decide that even though we can't see into the future and don't know what is going to happen, we are confident that God has something planned for us, the likes of which we cannot conceive. And because we trust in his love more than we can possibly trust in our partner's right now, we are trying to obey Christ's seemingly unsympathetic law about divorce.

God absolutely honors and rewards such faithfulness. Some of his most powerful signs and wonders take place in what look like irrevocably wrecked marriages. Creative energy once wasted on fantasizing, endless battling, or maintaining a secret life can now be spent on building a true partnership. Children who have been silently or not so silently suffering during years of unbroken siege are freed up to focus on their own vocations. And other struggling couples can find sustenance and hope in the obvious flourishing of a formerly cursed relationship.

how to begin the process

The first step in marital forgiveness is the same as in all other kinds of forgiving: we must have the will to do it. We must sincerely desire to forgive, and even to reconcile, though we may be very far from being capable of actually doing it. In the case of a third-party distraction, this step is effectively blocked unless we're willing to set aside the competing relationship long enough to deal with our spouse on the basis of reality.

Setting aside this other relationship is especially important because it is an ongoing source of hurt and shame to our partner that impedes his or her ability to forgive *us*. And, as psychologist and priest Morton Kelsey points out, it's extremely important in this early movement toward forgiveness to stop doing anything that might harm the other. If we find we have little will to do any of these things, then we need to pray for a strong desire to do what needs to be done to make forgiveness even possible.

The second step is to stop saying things that maintain the conflict. In marriages with children, this is critical. The temptation toward self-justification is tremendous, and kids provide a built-in, trusting audience for whatever we lay on them. As long as we are speaking ill of someone, however, it is literally impossible to forgive that person. Our mean-spirited words erect an impenetrable wall between us and the other person. And trashing someone else through speech simply feeds the sense of self-righteous indignation that must give way if our heart is to ever open. Yet habits of the tongue are often nearly impossible to break. After years of complaining about a spouse to relatives, children, or friends, it can be very difficult to shut up. Praying for the grace to be silent may become a daily task for a while.

Kelsey points to another kind of prayer that becomes key in the process of forgiving, and that is prayer directed specifically at the well-being of the person we're trying to forgive. It's one thing to stop harming our partner, another to stop speaking ill of him or her, and quite another to actually start praying for his or her health, welfare, and happiness. Yet it's impossible to keep hating a person we are sincerely praying for. Slowly but irrevocably, a specific kind of grace released by prayer begins to enter the life of that person, and also our own. It's a shared grace that helps soften the heart. I know couples who say that the most healing thing they did for their marriage was to begin praying out loud for one another.

With this kind of prayer, and with walls beginning to come down, it becomes much easier to
move from a position of resistance (bridling
the tongue) to creatively building up the other.
We consciously begin focusing on the gifts and
virtues of our partner, some of them hidden
from us for years. We pretend to be strangers,
meeting for the first time, and look for what is
good and what we can honestly admire. And we
mention these things out loud. Christianity has
always maintained a reverent awe for the power
of the spoken word. God, we believe, actually
spoke the world into existence. We can speak a
healthier, better spouse into existence too—not
through platitudes or manipulative sentimentality, but by really seeking the truth of who he or
she is, the truth that has been hidden from us by
our mutual animosity.

Finally, we wait patiently and in hope for
a transformative miracle. Grace comes to us
through the action of the Holy Spirit, and the
Spirit is, if nothing else, mysterious and even
whimsical. We cannot control where it goes
and what it does—we cannot command the

cleansing, renewing fire to come down on a relationship, no matter how ready we might be. But we can wait, prayerfully, and we can keep our eyes open and our hearts ready and available for what might happen next.

forgiving sins of the past

What about those who, like me, are already divorced? It's easy to look back and see what might have been done differently if I'd been living my life for God during that terrible and tumultuous time, instead of living for myself. But twenty-five years after the fact, it's clear that there's no going back. That marriage is irrevocably over and done.

Yet even for the already divorced, forgiveness and a certain kind of reconciliation are distinct possibilities. As I was amazed to find out when I finally got around to apologizing to my ex-husband, the reason he'd been able to go on with his life in such a healthy and productive way is that he'd taken the initiative and undergone the process of forgiving without my even having asked. He knew that both our lives, and the lives of our children, would be somehow crippled if we carried our sorrow, disappointment, guilt, and still-smoldering anger forward into the future.

The knowledge that I had been sincerely forgiven was, in part, what helped move me back to God. For the first time, I experienced the enormous relief and heady joy of being released from a burden of guilt and shame I fully deserved to carry the rest of my life. And that opened my closed heart to the possibility of confessing my sins to God and being absolved. Does this mean that nowadays I never feel the weight of that old shame and guilt? No—periodically, and usually during special family events, the two of them rise up before me like spectral mourners at a funeral. I'll never be rid of them, and that's as it should be.

Still, the release that came with knowing I was forgiven overshadows all this. My ex-husband's sincere expression of forgiveness showed me that the fine person I once cut to the quick was truly going to be all right. Those ugly open wounds were healing or had already healed, and though they would certainly leave scars, he'd emerged as a stronger and more loving human being. Because of his faith—faith he'd clung to for both our sakes—God had moved into the sad mess I created and made sure that all things really did work together for good. I can now look back and see how carefully God guided both of us through the dark valley of spiritual temptation and marital death and led us out into the light.

That sincere act of forgiveness on my ex-husband's part also continues to produce blessings in our divorced but reconciled relationship. Not only have we been able to share the joy of our children's big moments—graduation, marriage, childbirth—but we've also been able to witness the healing of myriad broken relationships that were a direct result of our divorce. For example, he was my siblings' beloved brother-in-law for thirteen years, and I was very close to his mother. Because of the complicated ties of loyalty that exist between blood relatives, these friendships were necessarily put into suspended animation when we split. People needed our tacit permission to resume them.

Last Thanksgiving, both extended families celebrated together at Mike's and my house, the first time we've gotten together without some kind of major event providing the reason. People seemed excited and pleased to have this opportunity to reconnect. Where I thought there might be tension or ice that required breaking, there was only a happy, warm buzz in the room. Folks had missed one another. The atmosphere was so upbeat that before we dived into the turkey, we actually joined hands and formed a large, if wavering, family circle.

Then we sang the doxology.

nine forgiving
in community

AFTER YEARS OF RETREATS at New Camaldoli Hermitage, I began to think seriously about becoming an oblate, or lay member, of this monastic community. I wasn't sure what such a step would entail—how does a busy wife and mother even *pretend* to be living by the Rule of St. Benedict, for example?—but I knew that my desire for a simpler, quieter, and more prayerful way of life was sincere and had been building for a long time.

I spoke with the oblate chaplain, who gave me a whole list of books to read and think about and told me to come back in twelve months or so, when I'd had time to reflect and pray about whether I was really being called to make the oblate vow. During that time of discernment, I read about the tenth-century St. Romuald of Ravenna, the founder of the Camaldolese order in Italy, and about the threefold Camaldolese charism of solitude, community, and martyrdom. I studied the Brief Rule of St. Romuald: "Sit in your cells as in a paradise. Put the whole world behind you and forget it. Watch your thoughts like a good fisherman watching for fish." I also studied the Benedictine Rule: "Therefore, we intend to establish a school for the Lord's service. In drawing up its regulations, we hope to set down nothing harsh, nothing burdensome." And most of all, I tried to imagine my whole responsibility-filled life being restructured on the basis of monastic values.

When my year of discernment was over, I felt surprisingly ready, and several days after Christmas, my friend Janet and I made our oblate vows before the assembled monks and congregation. Our loyal kids and husbands sat in the pews, no doubt secretly wondering what effect this ceremony would have on marriage and family life. At the end of the service, Janet and I processed around the circle of monks for brotherly hugs, had a happy lunch in the refectory, took some photos, and then headed back into the world.

We were in for a jarring transition.

Retreats were one thing—a momentary hiatus from our normal daily round—but joining the monastic community was quite another. *Every* day, including normal work hours and family obligations, was meant to be lived intentionally. We were to anchor ourselves in prayer, solitude, and silence, and we were to feed upon the Eucharist. Despite our jobs, our spouses and kids, and our long to-do lists, we were to learn to see the world in a whole new way. We were to become contemplatives.

After the high wore off, we ran into a block wall of reality. This new way of life was as difficult as it was lonely. Nobody else but Janet understood what it was like to want to—*need* to—slip off for some silent prayer or *lectio divina* (sacred reading) when unpaid bills littered the desk and dinner sat uncooked. No one else understood what a raucous enemy the phone had become. Worst of all was a nagging suspicion that even our most compassionate friends and relatives were convinced we'd become enslaved by an embarrassing midlife enthusiasm, as though we'd suddenly taken up yoga or cake decorating with a weird vengeance.

Thus, when Janet called one day with the news that several other oblates in our town were interested in forming a group, I was excited. Finally, a community of compatriots!

Our first meeting took place at the Old Mission in San Luis Obispo, and we were amazed to see how many other oblates lived in our area. We celebrated the morning office, Lauds, together, and we prayed and sang and listened to our speaker, one of the monks who'd driven down for the occasion. Then we shared a splendid potluck and celebrated the Eucharist. By the end of the day, we were ecstatic. It had suddenly come clear how we were going to do this seemingly impossible thing of being oblates in the world: we were going to lean upon *each other*.

The group honeymoon lasted almost three years. Every time we convened, we fell into one another's arms with happy cries of relief. It seemed that we were developing into true soul mates, shouldering burdens for each other, helping one another discern, inspiring and encouraging and blessing each other's lives. Gradually, the word got out, and other people—some who had not yet even visited the hermitage—began clamoring to come to our retreats. The Spirit was blowing throughout the land, or at least through San Luis Obispo County. This, I thought, was the church as it was meant to be.

Surely God was very, very pleased with us.

No sooner did I have this thought than the seed of a fierce, propriety pride in my own little spiritual community was planted and took root in my soul. Trouble wasn't far away.

the temptations of community

That building a good community is a process rife with dangers seems readily apparent in the Epistles of Sts. Paul, Peter, and James. Many of the letters they write to the infant congregations of their day specifically address the struggles of people from various ethnic groups, religious backgrounds, and social strata who are trying become a cohesive unit.

First, James warns about the tendency of Christian communities to inadvertently mirror societal values, particularly when it comes to the way they interact with the rich and powerful: "My brothers, show no partiality as you adhere to the faith in our glorious Lord Jesus Christ. For if a man with gold rings on his fingers and in fine clothes come into your assembly, and a poor person in shabby clothes also comes in, and you pay attention to the one wearing the fine clothes and say, 'Sit here, please,' while you say to the poor one, 'Stand there,' or 'Sit at my feet,' have you not made distinctions among yourselves and become judges with evil designs?" (Jms. 2:1–4). It seems that even the earliest Christians struggled with the temptation to flatter or in some way offer special homage to those with power and money—a clear departure from the picture of community as painted by

Jesus, which points his followers toward humble servanthood: "If I, therefore, as the master and teacher have washed your feet, you ought to wash one another's feet. I have given you a model to follow, so that as I have done for you, you should also do" (Jn. 13:14–15).

Why is it so important to avoid structuring religious communities on worldly patterns? Being told that we must kowtow to the rich and powerful as if we were still in the world can ignite envy, stir up hidden resentment, and destroy the possibility of true brotherhood and sisterhood. When we're brooding about our ranking in a group, we tend to become hypersensitive to perceived slights, particularly over leadership issues. We forget about St. Paul's beautiful image of the body and its distinct but essential parts. A lot of us would rather be the head than the foot, for example, whether or not we're suited for that position or called to it by God. Secret aspirations like these can cause us to sabotage the group.

A second way spiritual communities can get into trouble is through habitual wrangling.

St. Paul addresses the Corinthians about this problem: "When I came to you, brothers, proclaiming the mystery of God, I did not come with sublimity of words or of wisdom. For I resolved to know nothing while I was with you except Jesus Christ, and him crucified. I came to you in weakness and fear and much trembling, and my message and my proclamation were not with persuasive [words of] wisdom, but with a demonstration of spirit and power, so that your faith might rest not on human wisdom but on the power of God" (1 Cor. 2:1–5). St. Paul's reference to "human wisdom" indicates that he is addressing a very common problem among serious spiritual seekers: getting swept up in doctrinal or theological disputes that ultimately splinter the community of believers.

In his book *Discernment and Truth*, Mark McIntosh, a professor of systematic theology, asserts that when such disputes become endemic in a Christian community, we've failed the ultimate test of our faith: it's very clear that we're no longer loving one another as Christ loved us. More, our thinking can easily become clouded by an egoistic attachment to our own opinions. Not only do we risk losing what he calls "epistemological modesty," a basic virtue of an authentic intellectual life, but we ignore St. Paul's warning that without love, we're simply a "resounding gong or a clashing symbol" (1 Cor. 13:1). Our theological disputes become the point of our Christian identity; we're no longer worshiping God, but have made an idol of our own position.

What kinds of character traits are fostered by a disputatious religious atmosphere? Along with intellectual blindness, communities find themselves plagued by self-righteous finger-pointing, mean-spirited gossip, false accusations, suspicion of other people's motives, and mutual dislike—the antithesis of the loving unity to which Jesus calls his disciples.

A third warning from the apostles is against communities becoming presumptuous. James says, "Come, now, you who say, 'Today or tomorrow we shall go into such and such a town, spend a year there doing business, and make a profit'—you have no idea what your life will be like tomorrow. You are a puff of smoke that appears briefly and then disappears. Instead you should say, 'If the Lord wills it, we shall live to do this or that'" (Jms. 4:13–15). James is referring to a special problem among communities that have enjoyed, however briefly, a sure sense of the presence of the Holy Spirit, as my oblate group did for a time. The temptation in such a gratifying situation is toward what the Greeks would refer to as hubris (overweening pride) that comes from forgetting who is really directing things.

The presumption that follows is that we can somehow read the future and know what God has in store for us, and thus make elaborate plans on our own. The moment we feel our group has been specially blessed and is thus impervious to temptation, we are being presumptuous: no human community is invincible in this way. The vices that emerge in this kind of group are grandiosity, power struggles over whose vision should prevail, cruel disregard for those who seem to be overly traditional or without creative zest, and impatience with people who urge prayer and patience over quick, self-confident action.

Fourth, though the writers of the Epistles don't mention this particular danger, a special challenge for today's spiritual communities is our stake in self-fulfillment. We tend to judge marriages, friendships, and family relationships by how well they do or don't help us achieve that goal, and we measure communities by the same standard. Sometimes, for example, we join a group in order to get our emotional needs met. If we're lonely, we naturally long for companionship, so a group that turns out to be less friendly than we'd like will invariably cause us hurt. If, on the other hand, we're really seeking a community of like-minded people in order to fit in somewhere, we'll have a vested interested in group members thinking the same way we do—and are bound to be disappointed. Sometimes serious psychological problems are what prompt us to seek out a community; since most groups aren't qualified to deal with these, we're going to feel let down. And finally, even if we aren't looking for free counseling, we may still be more interested in personal fulfillment than in spiritual development. Though the two often overlap, they are not the same thing, and when we confuse them, we're fated to run into disappointment.

The great Puritan preacher Jonathan Edwards sums up in one hyphenated word what usually goes wrong with religious communities: unless they are very alert to the danger, they slowly become more rooted in *self-love* than in love of God. The Epistle writers make the same diagnosis. Self-love blinds us intellectually and spiritually, fosters sins such as envy, avarice, vainglory, pride, anger, spite, and contempt, and completely blocks the work of the Holy Spirit. Thus, the litmus test for any Christian community must be the love we bear for one another. This mutual love, when it exists, is proof that we really have given up our natural egoism and self-concern and put our hearts into the hands of God.

the first stormclouds for the oblate group

Given such a lengthy oblate honeymoon, I was ill-prepared for the abrupt transition, when it finally came, to a less heady but absolutely necessary stage of group life: the shift from fond hoping and dreaming to the real-life struggle to make a community work. The first indication that our group experience was about to change was a sudden drop-off in numbers of attendees for our retreats. Where had everybody gone? Some people moved away and lost contact. Others seemed simply to lose interest, and this was painful for me to accept. How could they stop caring about a group that meant so much to all of us? How could they sever a relationship with their own spiritual soul mates?

Then interpersonal problems began to surface—piques that, because I was so invested in the group succeeding, I at first refused to take seriously. One night after a retreat, for example, a prospective oblate called me, and in a voice shaking with emotion, demanded to know what I'd meant by a comment I directed her way during our discussion that day. I was floored. First, I didn't even remember making such a statement, and if I had, could not imagine how she'd interpreted it so personally. I was so taken aback, I actually chuckled, hoping she was making a joke. It was no joke, however, and she went on to accuse me of seeing her as weak and mentally unstable, someone who needed professional help. Someone who clearly didn't belong in the group.

Though I'd never given such a notion a moment's thought before, hearing the obvious anger in her voice and listening to her describe an ongoing series of put-downs on my part was both baffling and infuriating. How could she think such things of me? How long had she been hiding all this wrath under her sweet smile? This was the hardest part of all: I liked her as a human being, quite apart from her role as a potential fellow oblate. I thought she was pretty, smart, and droll, and I looked forward to her comments in the group. Her accusations made me feel callous and blind, and most of all, woefully naïve. All this time, I'd apparently been floating along on an insubstantial cloud of illusory group love.

I hung up the phone in a state of guilty anger. For the first time in three years, I was not looking forward to the next oblate meeting, especially if she were going to be there. Why did she have to ruin such a good thing? What was driving such a ridiculous accusation?

It did not cross my mind that she'd called to reveal something important to me, a secret she'd been unable to share with the group. She'd needed to show someone the appalling level of anxious insecurity that lay beneath her calm smile. Whether or not she consciously recognized this, she needed to lean on someone, and my comment had given her an excuse to open that discussion.

But I could not see any of this; I was too angry and upset, too disappointed at the sudden collapse of my beautiful fantasy about the oblate community. I could not forgive her for popping my bubble, and when other things began to go awry, I pinned part of the blame on her self-pity. Some months later, when she stopped coming to the group, I was privately relieved. Obviously, she'd been right the first time: she didn't belong.

Meanwhile, we oblates hosted a recreation day for the monks. Seven novices and the formation director arrived at our place the night before so that Mike could take some of them surfing in the morning. We sat around the campfire, eating pizza and getting to know each other, and the longer we talked, the more excited I became. A more promising group of young men would be hard to find, I thought: they were serious, intelligent, and well-educated, but also humorously self-deprecating and full of high spirits. More, these were young people who might reenergize the flagging oblate group. Their enthusiasm was infectious; how could we resist?

The following day, as more monks and oblates and neighbors showed up with their casseroles and salads and pies, I once again felt that old surge of happy, grateful certainty: this was the community I knew. These were my people. How could I have ever doubted the solidity and sheer goodness of this spiritual family of mine?

As I was setting up the kitchen for serving, one of the novices, Jerry, showed up in the doorway.

"Need any help?" he asked.

"Here," I said, handing him an apron and

pointing to the oven. "Why don't you start pulling out the hot stuff and setting it up on the butcher block?"

With his help, we were ready in no time. When I stepped out onto the porch and waved at the guys manning the barbeque, however, one of them held up ten fingers, so Jerry and I took off our aprons, poured some chips and salsa into bowls, took a couple of cold beers out of the fridge, and sat down at the breakfast nook to munch and wait. "It was great to meet all of you last night," I confessed. "You're a great group."

Jerry laughed. "Thanks," he said, "but you don't know what goes on behind the scenes."

"Well, I can guess," I told him. "It's not easy, becoming part of a community. I've been down that road myself."

"It's definitely been interesting. And I've gotten some great material out of it."

"Material?"

"You know—for my book."

"You're writing a book?"

"Yeah. That's why I wanted a chance to talk to you. I know you're a writer and I'm looking for a good agent. I thought maybe—well, maybe you could introduce me or something."

I carefully laid my chip back in the bowl. "I don't get it, Jerry. How are you going to become a monk when you've got a book project going? Aren't you going to find it distracting?"

He took another swallow of beer, set the bottle at arm's length, then glanced around to see if anyone were within earshot. "Look," he said earnestly, leaning closer. "I'm a writer, not a monk. I'm here for two years—that's it. Then I've got some other things going."

"Do *they* know that?"

He shook his head. "It would ruin it," he said. "If they knew I wasn't serious. I'm trying to get the true flavor, you know what I mean? You've got to be on the inside to get the true flavor."

I stared at him, a bright young man filled with ambition—someone a lot like I had once been—and found that I couldn't feel anger at his crass self-interest, only disappointed sorrow.

He was not without sensitivity, however, and he could see by my face what I thought of his plan. "Look," he objected. "I'm trying for

Columbia. I'm going to need a great portfolio. Do you know how hard it is to get into their writing program?"

I nodded sadly. "I do," I said. "But don't string out the monks any longer. They need to know."

"Right," he said, pushing back his chair and standing up. "I thought you, of all people, would understand." And a week later, he left the community without telling them why.

The disappointments with oblate life were not over, however. Our beloved oblate chaplain was given a different set of responsibilities at the hermitage. His replacement, equally beloved, got cancer and died within the year at age fifty-six, leaving us mournful and bereft and focused on our own mortality. Somebody who refused the official role of lay group leader nevertheless kept trying to run the show. Where we had once enjoyed a blissful sense of unity, it seemed to me that we were quickly dividing into unacknowledged factions and alliances. And people kept quitting, over one hurt or another.

One day I realized that I, too, was emotionally done with the group. A spiritual community was a volatile thing, much more so than I'd ever suspected, and I was worn out with the interpersonal dynamics. Where I had once felt nothing but a childlike, joyous love for my fellow oblates, I now found myself suspiciously looking for evidence that at least some people were using the group for their own ends: as a platform for their own idiosyncratic opinions, a care center for their emotional wounds, an escape from their real-life responsibilities. Most of all, I was disillusioned to the point of doubting the promises of the Gospels. If we, as monastic oblates, could not get it together as a loving community, then who could?

Depressed, I met with Father Robert, a former prior at the hermitage, and asked him the same question. How did the monks work through all these complexities? To put it in the most basic terms, how did they find a way to forgive and keep on loving each other?

We were sitting in a room off the bookstore on a bone-chilling gray day. The radiator, which was filling the room with blessed heat, snapped and chimed and hissed against the recorded chanting from the next room. Father Robert listened to my litany of woes, his head cocked birdlike to one side, then gave me one of his deceptively gentle and unassuming smiles— "deceptive" because Father Robert is sharper than the sharpest tack, and has a way of getting directly to the heart of the matter so quickly that I am always finding myself bushwhacked by his incisive wisdom. "Oh, my," he clucked. "All that can be *so* tiring and disillusioning, and don't I know it. But you see, we must never give up on love, and one way to do that is to minimize the occasions for disagreement."

I gave him a wary look—where was he going with this?—and shoved my rocking chair a little closer to the radiator, which was finally managing to thaw me out.

"By that I mean, we try not to open discussions that will automatically lead to conflict. In this community we have people with a whole array of political and religious opinions. You'd be amazed! For instance, we have people who watch Mother Angelica every day living side by side with people who are exploring interfaith dialogue with the Buddhists and Taoists. You see? And that can lead to infighting unless we deliberately curtail those kinds of discussions. Everything is directed, as much as possible, to what actually unifies us."

"Which is?" I asked, though of course I already knew the answer, just not how to implement it.

"Prayer. Praying together in church every day. Praying for each other's well-being and forgiving each other."

"Well, of course," I said, "but what about *us?* What about a group that doesn't live together in the same place, doesn't worship in the same church each day, and only meets every few months? How do you keep the mutual prayer thing going with a group like *that*?"

He shook his head. "Very challenging," he said. "You certainly have your work cut out for you, don't you?"

Well, yes we do indeed, I thought, a bit miffed, and that's the whole problem, isn't it? But then, feeling myself getting warmer and warmer thanks to that blessed radiator and— let's face it—Father Robert's gentle, quizzical, irresistible smile, I thought, but maybe this is the job of the oblates, our whole vocation as a community. Not to be some kind of holy icon for the world, not to show up the institutional church with our magnificent loving ways, but simply to hold one another in constant prayer and see what comes out of *that*. I began to try out the new plan as soon as I got home from the hermitage.

the need for forgiveness

My prayer experiment produced almost instant results. I found, to my surprise, that I was *unable* to pray, no matter how I tried, for certain people in the group, people I felt had been particularly irresponsible in some way, or even outright destructive. I would visualize their faces, say their names out loud, and . . . nothing. I couldn't even shape the words. Soon, I was apologizing all over the place to God for this curious lack of ability to pray for these folks. What was going on?

I'd just run into an implacable fact about praying for others: we can't pray for them if we are at the same time unwilling to forgive them. We are stuck on the flypaper of unresolved anger, and every time we generate an image of their faces or try to say their names out loud, what comes to us is not prayer but a surge of powerful emotion: rage, hurt, a sense of being falsely accused, the conviction we've been let down and it's not our fault.

For quite some time, I tried to wriggle around on that flypaper without actually going through the painful enterprise of ripping myself free. But prayer for these people was thoroughly blocked as long as I remained stuck in past wounds. And there was an even worse problem to contend with: the community as a whole. I needed to forgive that too—the whole group at the same time—for not being the vibrant spiritual dynamo I had once dreamed of. The collective nature of community makes forgiveness all the more complicated. It's not enough to forgive the individuals involved: we must also figure out a way to forgive what they represent, which in the case of spiritual communities is no less than our highest aspirations.

Diadochus of Photike, a fifth-century bishop, recommends a focus on the generosity of God as the best antidote against anger toward the community. When we focus on God and what he is doing, we stop looking to the group as a vehicle for magnificent and fantastical accomplishments. When we focus on God's generosity toward the world, we immediately run into the fact of his generosity toward *us*, personally—we run into the fact of his mercy, his patience, his steady love. We remember his willingness to trust us despite our frailty. We recall his refusal to trap us in our own pasts. And we realize that our little community, so fractious and so troublesome, so disillusioning and so tiresome, is nothing more than a microcosm of what God deals with every day in his munificent generosity.

Surely, we can be a little more generous toward the few people who make up our group? Surely, we can give some credit, cut some slack, relax, and learn to delight in the aggravating complexities generated by people of good will, trying to make a go of it together?

Thinking of God's generosity, as Diadochus of Photike recommends, turned out to be an important step for me in my relationship to the oblate community. Jesus tells the parable of the ungrateful servant who is forgiven a great debt by his master, then turns around and gouges someone beneath him who owes him a pittance. I thought about this parable and its very clear message the next time I tried to pray for a group member and found myself still stymied by my lack of forgiveness. Forgiving in community is in many ways the same thing as forgiving parents, spouses, or other family members. It is just as hard, if not harder, and it requires that the same basic desire be present in us in order to get the process off the ground.

We must, first of all, honestly desire to forgive—in this case, not only the individuals in the group, but the group as a whole. If we can't yet locate this desire in ourselves—where, oh where, could it be hiding?—then this is where the prayer project begins: "Lord, please help me *want* to forgive this person or group."

Second, we must consciously begin to change our way of thinking about the community or the people in it. We must stop brooding over disillusionment or wounds, thinking negative thoughts (e.g., this group is now too *boring* to worry about), or fantasizing about how much better it could be if only we were in charge of the world.

Third, we must stop saying negative things about the group. We must stop all our complaining, our bitter gossip to members of our particular faction, and our dreary predictions for the future. We must find and cling to hope, and our words about the group and its prospects must spring from that theological virtue rather than from our own soured point of view.

Fourth, we must stop in the middle of everything and make a private vow of stability. We can't go through all the effort of forgiving if the back door is standing wide open. A key virtue in monasticism is staying put, for community, which is neither inherited like family nor romantically energized like marriage, requires more than a little loyalty in order for the group to survive.

Fifth, we must assiduously avoid the mistake of believing "once forgiven, always forgiven." Groups in particular require ongoing forgiveness—as Jesus puts it, forgiveness seventy times seven—and we may literally have to forgive the same person for the same annoying trait over and over and over again until we're ready to scream . . . and then forgive him or her again. As another longtime monk, Father Bernard, once told me, "It is not the big thing but the small things, repeated over and over, that become a water torture for us. Like the man with a cold who can never remember to bring a supply of Kleenex to church with him."

Sixth, we must ask for the strength to resist a particular temptation of group membership, which is to complicate the situation with impossible-to-meet objectives. It is hard enough for people in groups simply to stay friends. The higher our demands on everyone, the more often we'll be disappointed, hurt, or disillusioned. Forgiving the group means consciously letting go of idealistic, unrealistic aspirations about how it is to develop, what it is to do, and how much it is going to change the world. Forgiving the group means allowing room for all the human foibles that invariably lurk beneath the surface, waiting to spring out.

Finally, to forgive our community, we must learn to bless it—day after day, week after week, year after year. Along with praying for the ongoing power to forgive, we should be asking for an infusion of the Holy Spirit. When the Spirit has already been and gone, as happened in the case of our oblate group, we need to beg for its return. Jesus promises, "Wherever two or three are gathered together in my name, there I am in the midst of them" (Mt. 18:20), and we can count on this, no matter how fractured or distressed the group may seem. Jesus is there, ready to bless us as a community, if we will only remember to call upon him.

At the end of my conversation with Father Robert, I raised what I saw as the most significant issue in terms of our oblate group: we'd never been through a real formation program, the kind of spiritual "boot camp" each novice monk must undergo. Despite all our reading and discussing, we hadn't yet been "formed," and maybe this was our real problem: we were still far too individualistic to become a truly harmonious community. "I do see," he said thoughtfully. "However, we think the best tool for formation is the community itself. When you *have* to get along with one another, you quickly find areas that need improvement in yourself. And isn't it providential, what a variety of people you have in your group! You can all help form one another in no time at all!"

I had to admit, this thought had never occurred to me.

The eleventh-century spiritual master Symeon the New Theologian reminds us that the point of the Christian life is ultimately not how we perform but who we become: "And in the future life a Christian will not be tested as to whether he renounced the world, whether he fasted, whether her performed vigils, whether he prayed, whether he wept, or performed any other such good deeds in this present life; but he will be carefully tested as to whether he has some kind of likeness to Christ, as a son to his father."

Trying to live in imitation of Jesus can be a daunting proposition. One way to start is to look at how he spent his time. When we do, it strikes us that he was completely invested in others, whether these people were his family or fellow villagers, his disciples, or the vast crowds he taught in the synagogues and in the open air. Even when he appeared to be slipping away for some solitude, he was not escaping into himself; instead, he was communing with his Abba. He was tending his relationship with God. If Jesus is our model, it's clear that the Christian life must ultimately work itself out in community. And what protects and sustains community life is none other than merciful love and forgiveness.

part 4
being forgiven

*seeking and accepting
mercy for ourselves*

ten when we
are at fault

AFTER MY LONG-AGO DIVORCE and remarriage, and while I was still in the grip of anger, depression, fear, and guilt, everything in life seemed to be mockingly reflecting back the turmoil within. I could not be grateful for what I now had—I was too fearful of losing what I'd fought so hard to obtain. I could not surrender my will to God—I was too afraid of facing up to my sin.

Instead of romantic bliss, Mike and I were dealing with four little kids who had not chosen their new stepfamily and, if consulted, would have certainly passed up the opportunity to be in it. Instead of the extended honeymoon state I had fondly envisioned, we were dealing with the stark reality of divorce-caused debt. The ongoing stress was beginning to drive a wedge between us. Had I gone through all this sorrow, loss, and guilt only to have this new marriage gradually destroyed too? In this bitter frame of mind, I decided to go back to college and complete the work for my unfinished degree. And it was there on campus, long before I had any sense that God was in pursuit of me—his lost and angry lamb—that I met my first spiritual mentor.

A wise mentor can be invaluable during a major life transition like the one I was just entering. Transitions are all about moving on from the past, and often we are not yet ready to let the past go, no matter how tumultuous or painful it has been. In my case, I only knew myself against the backdrop of my personal history, so giving up the past meant giving up part of my self-identity. Yet the ugly memories I couldn't stop clutching to my bosom were slowly killing my hope for the future. What I needed was a kind of soul doctor, someone able to "read" what had gone wrong spiritually and to prescribe a cure. But I also needed to have my old, childish misperceptions about God dismantled before I could acknowledge the desperate quality of my situation and accept help.

In this first mentor of mine, I found someone who could handle both jobs. A philosophy professor, he taught the history of ethics to general education students who often resented having to take the course. Not for long, however. He knew just how to get our undivided attention; he turned the required readings into an occasion for moral self-examination. Though he never revealed his Christianity in class, he was pointing us in the direction of God without our knowing it. Despite my angry inner turmoil, I was riveted by the readings and lectures in that course. After many years of trying to run my life without God, I began to understand that there was a direct connection between my anger, sorrow, disappointment, and guilt, and my long-ago repudiation of Christianity. Once I got a taste of what I was missing, I could not get enough of it.

I began visiting my professor's office after class nearly every day. Armed with a list of urgent questions—questions that I'd put on hold as a teenager disgusted with God's seeming inability to banish suffering—I argued and prodded and pontificated my way back to faith. Thus began a years-long spiritual mentorship with a man who brooked no nonsense. If I were going to get better, if I were going to give up my resentment and become a real disciple of Christ, then I had to work at it. First of all, I had to learn how to think rather than simply emote my way through life. Then I had to steep myself in Scripture and tradition. Finally, I had to give up my pride, the pride that had for so long insisted I could go it alone and didn't need God.

My mentor was relentlessly honest and tough with me. He could see me better than I could see myself, and what he saw apparently alarmed him, or at least seemed to convince him that I couldn't afford a lengthy rehabilitation. It was time to get cracking, and I did, entering into an intense reconstruction project I could never have undergone without being fairly desperate to see real change in myself.

This fast track was exactly what I needed. In fact, I believe it saved my life. It certainly helped save my already imperiled second marriage. And ultimately, it created a structure in our lives that helped Mike regain his own lost faith. Satan, however, doesn't back off when we are trying to get closer to God. He redoubles his efforts at such times. And my essential rebelliousness, that prideful need to run my own show that had gotten me in so much trouble in the past, had not yet been broken, but merely gone underground, already seeking a way to reassert itself.

For several years before that happened, however, I was able to start looking honestly at the havoc I had caused in other people's lives. At first I could not fathom what lay at the heart of this destructive behavior of mine. Under the prodding of my mentor, however, I began to discern the outlines of my particular self-deceiving lie, the story I told myself to avoid feeling shame. The story had to do with being a misunderstood child, an unappreciated wife, a thwarted artist, and an academic misfit. Nobody, it seemed, understood how hard it was to be me. *But* (I protested self-defensively) I had a right to be loved and happy, just like everyone else, and so I set out to get what was rightfully mine.

With my mentor's help, I began to make the connection between my self-pity and my sinning. A good spiritual guide can often see what we, in our plagued blindness, cannot. The image of light breaking into darkness appears many times throughout the New Testament; one function of this inbreaking light is to bring into focus that which is obscure or unfathomable. Ironically, what is often shrouded in the deepest darkness is the state of our own soul. Once I could finally take in the bigger picture—that for nearly 100 percent selfish reasons, I'd hurt innocent people, people I loved—I was filled with dismay.

When we finally catch a glimpse of what's been right under our noses all along, dismay is common. Sometimes the emotional response is more dramatic—we find ourselves shocked and horrified, even distraught. Yet this shock can plant within us a new attitude or resolution that leads to genuine change. The experience of being cut to the heart so deeply that our whole orientation shifts is known as *compunction*. Repentance for the injuries we've inflicted on ourselves, other people, and God often brings with it the mournful tears of compunction and an overwhelming longing to be forgiven.

seeking forgiveness

However, *wanting* to be forgiven is different than actually having to go out and seek it. The first person I approached for forgiveness was my sister Gail, who in many ways is as close to me as a twin. My teenaged repudiation of God in Honduras caused our first and only real rift. Gail is what the nineteenth-century psychologist William James refers to as "once-born," a person who comes into the world as a believer and never seems to undergo the existential angst and troubling doubts the rest of us usually face. Once-born people are not simply passive or complacent, though; they are instead completely oriented toward God from the time they open their eyes. They are God's steadfast lovers.

My angry teenaged agnosticism thus came as a distressing surprise to the once-born girl who adored her big sister. And over the years, hoping and praying I'd change my mind, she never stopped raising the issue when she had a chance. When as a young wife and mother I confessed to her that I was falling in love with Mike, she was even more devastated. Not only did she adore my first husband, she was worried for my soul. I knew she was praying for me—she told me so—and I resented it. I didn't want anybody trying to rope God into the situation; I didn't even believe in him anymore.

Besides, my life philosophy was now different than it had been when we were growing up together in the Lutheran Church. Love, even illicit love, could not be wrong, I asserted—not when there was so much hatred and evil in the world. How could she criticize me for loving somebody when people were out there having wars?

For several years, she tried to talk me out of leaving my marriage. She never tried to argue with me—she was always respectful when she brought the issue to the floor—but that didn't matter. Emboldened by her "silly faith," she felt she had the right to criticize me, and as far as I was concerned, *nobody* did that. My life was my own business.

When she persisted, I lashed out at her, heaping scathing accusations against Christianity upon her head. I implied that she was a gullible, naïve child if she couldn't see how morally bankrupt the church had become. What were all the loving Christians doing, for example, when slavery became a way of life in the Bible Belt? Where was the church when women were struggling for basic rights? During these diatribes, she would listen quietly, slowly going pale with sorrow at my implacable resentment toward religion. Then she would go back to praying for me, which drove me nuts.

The night I finally left my first husband, I found myself collapsed in a weeping heap on the floor of my new apartment. What was I doing? How could I go through with this? What would happen with the kids? How would we all survive? Automatically, I called Gail, crying into the receiver, and told her where I was. She drove from another town at midnight to be with me, begging me to reconsider, then staying up the rest of the night, praying on her knees in another room.

But by morning, I was as steely as ever—and resentful of the fact that she'd stayed and prayed. Much as I loved her, she was an obstacle in my way. I didn't need prayer; I needed the guts to start a new life, and my praying sister was nothing but an impediment. I told her to go, that I was fine now and needed to be alone.

But now, years later, I finally had an inkling of the hurt I'd caused her. So when we were visiting the family for Thanksgiving that fall, I asked her to go for a walk with me, just the two of us. We set out into the hills above my brother's house, puffing steam in the cold November air. As she strode along beside me, talking of other things, I realized with a jolt of shame that, since the day it happened, she had never mentioned that awful night in the apartment, or ever shown any anger toward me for my arrogant ways.

"Gail," I said, stopping in the middle of the trail and putting my hand on her arm. "I have something to say to you."

One reason we've always been so close as sisters is that she knows how to "read" me; among the various talents in our large family, her special gift is a highly developed intuition that is both endearing and exasperating. "What?" she asked, innocently enough, but I could tell by the look in her eyes that she suspected what was up: I was about to make some sort of self-important speech.

I didn't want to speechify; I wanted to apologize and ask her for forgiveness. But my tongue felt stuck in my throat. I was embarrassed, ashamed, already looking for a way to escape the situation I'd set up myself. She could sense that. "Paula," she said softly, patting my hand where it lay on her forearm, "what's wrong?"

being forgiven

Despite the genuine remorse I felt, and despite my longing to be forgiven, I suddenly felt afraid of what would happen next. Would she, could she, *truly* forgive someone she loved who'd treated her so cruelly? Would my bringing these old painful memories out into the light of day interject embarrassed awkwardness into our longtime, comfortable relationship? Would she suddenly reveal a hidden anger I'd never suspected? Entering the landscape of forgiveness was like entering a vast wilderness with no road signs in it. But now that I'd raised the issue, I had to go through with it.

So I apologized—stiffly, formally, even a tad resentfully. Apologizing for doing wrong felt like admitting, in public, that I had screwed up. I was voluntarily acknowledging that I didn't know everything after all, that sometimes I made mistakes—big ones—and that no matter how "good" I thought I was, I caused people pain. To have to look into Gail's gentle eyes and reveal all this felt like a major comedown. No longer could I maintain the undisputed, lofty position of revered elder sister that I'd occupied in her life since she was born. My apology didn't simply equalize things between us; it put me in a morally inferior position. I could feel myself shrinking with shock, as though I'd just, for no good reason whatsoever, leapt naked into icy water.

She listened thoughtfully to my reluctant admission that I hadn't respected her much during that time, that I thought she was a gullible fool for her steadfast loyalty to God, that I'd discounted as Christian propaganda almost everything that came out of her mouth. Then she confessed, "Yes, that hurt, all right. It hurt a lot. But what hurt more was worrying about you—what was going to happen to you. How you were ever going to get over your anger at God and the world. *That's* what made me cry sometimes." Then she gave me a tremulous smile and patted my hand again. "I forgive you," she said. "I forgave you back then. But thanks for apologizing."

"You're welcome," I said gruffly, but inside I was feeling alarmingly shaky. With that pat on the hand and those words of forgiveness, she'd just broken through my defenses in a way that made me feel intensely vulnerable, and I found that scary. Somehow, being forgiven by my sister had set my old, comfortable, self-justifying lies into an entirely new perspective. The experience of being forgiven had revealed even more clearly my secret apparatus for elevating the self in every circumstance. I could no longer look toward my wounds as justifying causes of my bad behavior without having to admit the dishonesty of that strategy. Her loving act of forgiveness had shown me up for what I was: not strong and self-sufficient at all, but dependent and weak, in constant need of mercy and grace. And though I was grateful for her magnanimity, much of this felt just plain awful.

However, my sister had actually made things easy for me. By refusing to allow my transgressions to fracture or destroy our relationship, she'd eliminated a major complicating factor in most forgiveness situations: anger and recrimination. I never felt rejected, shunned, or judged by her, so even though it was difficult to publicly admit guilt, I never had to overcome self-defensiveness or deep hurt at the loss of our friendship. I could look clearly and honestly at what I'd done and say the words that needed to be said. We had no need to reconcile; nothing between us had ever been destroyed.

Most situations requiring forgiveness are far more complicated. We hurt someone who then quite naturally responds with anger or withdraws in pain. Our first reaction to their emotional response is often denial; we are not at fault, we assure ourselves—they are merely over-reacting. Then, as the relationship continues to deteriorate, the full ramifications of our actions begin to sink in.

The resulting impetus to seek forgiveness is usually twofold: not only do we feel moral guilt for our transgressions, as I did over the mean things I once said to Gail, but we also feel worry about the devastating harm we have caused the relationship. To truly feel forgiven in situations like these, we seem to need a corresponding twofold response from the person we have injured: both absolution and a willingness to reconcile. If these are not immediately forthcoming, it's easy to become bitter and walk away. A broken relationship vastly compounds the difficulty of seeking forgiveness and accepting it when it is finally offered.

After all the work I had done to get to a place where I could seek forgiveness from my sister, I found myself facing a broken relationship with my mentor. Despite all the help I'd gotten from him during the critical transition from agnosticism back to faith, a little piece of me was still off in the corner, sulking over the rigorous self-examination he'd put me through. The experience of being cut to the heart through compunction is a painful one, and when the shock is administered by another person, he or she can become a convenient target for wounded pride. In time, I found myself resenting the man who could never be buffaloed by my charm or my accomplishments—who, when asked for his opinion about how I was doing, merely pointed out that there was plenty left to tackle. In a rebellious mood, I said some nasty things, calculated to get a rise. Then I said a few more. And within a matter of months, I'd managed to knock to pieces a truly life-changing relationship.

the five stages of grief

In their book, *Healing Life's Hurts,* Dennis and Matthew Linn use Elisabeth Kübler-Ross's five stages of grief to describe what happens when we find ourselves grappling with the self-caused loss of a major relationship. First, we go into denial. What happened either hasn't happened at all, or it isn't nearly as bad as we first thought it was. The shock of loss is too hard to bear all at once, so we go into a self-protective shell.

The second stage of grieving a damaged relationship is anger. We blame everyone but ourselves for the wound. There is no way *we* can be at fault, though something is bitterly wrong. When we seek an alternative to self-justifying wrath, however, we find ourselves descending into sorrow, and we're not ready for that yet. It's far more satisfying to dwell on the sins of the person we've hurt, turning the inevitable human weaknesses we uncover during this long and hostile analysis into evidence that he or she was surely asking for it.

Yet anger is wearing and, if we're going about our Christian business, unsustainable. How can we be reading the Bible, praying, going to church, and pursuing a life in Christ while nursing settled rage? The answer is, we can't, so we try something new. Kübler-Ross's third step in the grief process is called "striking bargains." We say things to God such as, "If you will show that man the error

of his ways and instruct him to *admit* it, then I
am willing to offer an apology. If you will soften
her hard heart, I will graciously agree to once
again be her friend." This bargaining stage can
last for quite some time and become extremely
creative. However, we are still refusing to feel true
contrition—we are still holding out. We are only
willing to let go of the hurt on our own terms.
We want a certain kind of satisfaction before
we're willing to look honestly and humbly at our
own culpability.

Once we realize we can't change the situation
through bargaining with God, we tend to slip
into sadness or even depression. Psychologists
believe that depression is anger turned on
ourselves, and this is certainly what it feels
like. Where before, self-righteous energy kept
us going, now we sink into despondency and
genuine sorrow. We have hurt someone we
love. We have idiotically destroyed a marvelous
relationship—a difficult relationship, for sure,
but nevertheless, truly marvelous. We have
spurned a gift, crushed a flower, spit in the face
of something good.

I passed through all five stages of grief before I could see that at the root of the broken relationship with my former mentor lay the same old pride that had plagued me since childhood, the pride that insisted I was always right, that I knew what was best for myself, and that I even knew what was best for others. But now I'd run entirely out of theories and plans for how to run the world. For years, Mike had fondly said to me whenever he caught me staring blankly out the window, "I can hear your wheels spinning." I realized that this constant thinking of mine was in part what had led me into this spiritual dead end. I always had to figure things out on my own. I couldn't imagine simply stopping and waiting for God to tell me what to do next.

a communique from God

Somewhere during this sad time, Mike and I went camping on a northern lake. We were the only people in the park, and the forest was hushed and very dark. At some point in the middle of the night, I suddenly awoke from a sound sleep, as though someone had called my name. I pulled back the curtain of the trailer window and looked out at the lake, which lay shimmering under a cascade of silver moonlight. But it wasn't the moonlight that caught my attention; it was the black water: deep, mysterious, and silent.

In a flash, I realized that, just like Peter, I was being called to get out of my bed and walk across that water. I was being called to enter, through faith alone, into a great mystery. And if I heeded that call, nobody could accompany me. This was something I had to do on my own. This was a frightening thought, but in an odd way, reassuring too.

The next morning I woke understanding that in this painfully broken relationship, I was dealing with something far beyond my ability to understand or analyze or control. To allow myself to finally give way to God and others and to allow myself to be forgiven would take courage and humility I did not have. The only thing I could do was pray for help in overcoming my fear of the unknown—my fear of giving up autonomy.

Kübler-Ross says that the final stage of grief—how wounded relationships finally heal—is acceptance. Until we get to the place of peaceful, anticipatory waiting for whatever God has in store for us next, we remain stuck. Though I wasn't even sure anymore that I knew how to pray at all, I confessed to God that I was worthless without him and that he could do whatever he liked with me; I promised not to resist anymore. As soon as I prayed that prayer, I was flooded with a quiet peace. No new insights hit me, and I still could not imagine any sort of good resolution to the broken relationship, but that was okay. My job was to wait in hope.

As the days went on and I continued to reiterate my promise to let God work in this situation, on one level I found it very easy to stop thinking about it at all. When I "checked in" with it during daily prayer, it seemed to have no greater importance than anything else in my life. I prayed a simple prayer that if God wanted it healed, then I trusted him to make that happen. If the time wasn't right yet, or perhaps it would be better left as it was, then I trusted him in that too. As in the dark forest that night, there was a curious, anticipatory hush in the air that showed me what I'd been missing all those years I tried to control my relationships instead of allowing God to have his way with me. I could only sense this now because I was living, perhaps for the first time in my life, in a right relationship with God. I was no longer mistaking the *mysterium tremendum* for myself. I had learned about awe, which is a necessary condition for obtaining spiritual knowledge.

Even with this new understanding, what I didn't fully realize yet is that until I reached this stage of acceptance and willingness to obey God without reserve, I hadn't been *ready* to be forgiven by my wounded brother. Until this moment, all of my thinking had been essentially self-centered, and thus I was incapable of honestly asking for forgiveness. I had been far more concerned about losing a valuable relationship than I was about the sin of pride that had caused me to destroy it in the first place. My motivation was not love, but egoism.

When Jesus tells his followers they must assume they are at fault when someone is angry with them, he deliberately counteracts our tendency toward this kind of egoism—our tendency to blithely assume our own innocence, regardless of all evidence to the contrary. Just as we can't be trusted to pass judgments against others without being tempted to elevate ourselves, we're often completely unaware of the way we come across to the rest of the world. Even if we have some inkling, we many times grossly underestimate the effect of our words and behavior.

Thus, it doesn't matter whether or not we "meant anything by it," or whether in our opinion the person we've hurt is overly sensitive, or even whether he or she "deserved" the nasty rebuff or snub. Assuming we are at fault is the best way to avoid the much more serious error of assuming we're not when we are. This is why Christ tells his disciples that if they are bringing a gift to the altar and realize their brother is angry with them, they must stop, go seek him out, and do their best to reconcile before they make their offering. They must always err on the side of love.

Our personal relationships are like mirrors that reflect back our level of intimacy with God. We cannot presume to relate to him unless we know how to relate to our fellow human beings. The First Letter of John puts this very succinctly: "If anyone says, 'I love God,' but hates his brother, he is a liar; for whoever does not love a brother whom he has seen cannot love God whom he has not seen" (1 Jn. 4:20). Consider the flipside of this teaching: if anyone says "I love God" but is not ready or able to accept forgiveness for the wounds he inflicts on others through his own imperfection, he, too, may be a liar.

Christ's insistence that we do our best to reconcile with a wounded brother, regardless of who did what to whom, is a strong reminder that we cannot say we love God while continuing to live in enmity with others. This means we must learn to forgive, and learn to be forgiven; in most broken relationships, both are necessary before reconciliation becomes a possibility. Forgiveness is the way we begin to heal the sin-caused divisions between us. But, as was true in my case, often we must go through a long period of "waiting on the Lord" for the ground to be fully prepared. It takes truly serious, ongoing harm to damage or destroy a major relationship; our rush toward reconciling before the time is right can only delay the process.

In my situation, that wait was more than worth it. Not only did it force me to start letting go of my tight, controlling grasp on God and other people, but it allowed me to accept with joy and relief—rather than with the old, secret resentment—the forgiveness of my wounded friend when it was finally offered. And because the wound had been allowed to heal in its own time, blessed reconciliation followed.

eleven from wounded
to healed

NOT LONG AFTER HONDURAS and my first marriage at nineteen, I began thinking about having babies. I gave birth to my daughter when I was twenty-four, and to my son less than a year and a half later. Both of them arrived near the end of the seventies, when natural childbirth and breastfeeding were the way to go. Before I went into labor the first time, I read everything I could find about how to handle mega-pain without drugs and prepared myself for delivery like an athlete going into major competition.

Perhaps because I was wide awake and thus got the full childbirth experience, complete with sweating, moaning, grunting, mewling, and hoarse, desperate breathing, both babies seemed like survival miracles to me. How could they be so exquisite, so astonishingly *healthy,* after that brutal marathon we'd just been through? What harm had I already done to them without wanting to or meaning to?

This helpless question—what have I *done* to you?—would become a kind of mantra during their infancy, toddlerhood, and elementary school years. My mothering skills didn't come naturally, or at least it didn't seem so to me, who felt very young and inexperienced in the face of these two almost twins, both so bright and curious and adventurous. When I wasn't worrying about feeding and sleeping issues, I was stewing over the possibility of illness or accident or inflicting psychological trauma. This worry was partly guilt-generated, for along with being a mother, I was already an ambitious young writer, striving mightily to be published as often as possible. My fretting about the kids seemed coincidentally tied to the amount of time I spent at the typewriter.

I left the marriage when they were in kindergarten and first grade, which amplified that guilty worry a hundredfold. As I had before they were born, I read everything I could find on children from split families. I studied the statistics and consulted the experts, but nothing I dug up helped in any way. The facts seemed very clear; no child escaped the divorce experience unscathed. Through my decision to move out, I had doomed them in ways that would not necessarily become apparent for decades.

Thus, that early mantra—what have I done to you?—came to color almost everything about my relationship with my kids. I scrutinized them for signs of depression, anxiety, concealed rage. Every time one of them ran a fever, I sat beside the bed, studying the flushed, sleeping face and delicate fan of eyelashes, thinking, "There is pure and shining innocence, which I have destroyed." If they got hurt, it was because I had not been vigilant enough: I was too busy mulling over the short story I was writing, or I was caught up in the high drama of our economic woes. Or (more likely) if they got hurt, it was because I was divorced, and they were therefore, by definition, hurting all the time.

This is not to say they weren't. But, as they told me much later, their hurts were more private than what I imagined, and weren't always connected with my motherly failures at all. More than that, they were both naturally brave children, and they were bravely taking on their new way of life in ways I kept missing, for my vision was blocked by this unrelenting guilt.

One time, for example, when my son was nine, I made an ill-conceived attempt to apologize to him for all the turmoil I'd caused in his young life with the love affair and divorce. I thought that if only I could say I was sorry, and if only he could bring his small self to forgive me, I might finally be released from the grinding pain around my heart. But he was nervously appalled at the direction our conversation seemed to be headed, and told me he "really didn't want to talk about it." Then he gave me a quick, tight hug and leapt out of the car as though devils were after him.

Despite the stalwart sturdiness of my children, no doubt obvious to everyone but me, that mantra, with its attendant emotional train of guilt, shame, and persistent unease, became part of an obsessive thought pattern. No matter what I did, no matter how I tried, I could not help myself: whenever I looked at my kids, I saw, hovering like a malign aura around their bright heads, the dark shape of my many sins. Neither my rebellious pride, normally so quick to leap to my defense, nor my self-deceptive lies could get me past the stark reality that I had hurt those beautiful babies that had been the sun and moon to me. At the root of my pervasive self-pity lay this seemingly untreatable shame and guilt.

held captive by our wounds

Psychiatrist and spiritual director Gerald May writes about what it's like to be enslaved to such obsessive thought patterns. In his book *Addiction and Grace,* he asserts that any time we lose our ability to stop doing or thinking something, regardless of how much we'd like to quit, we are addicted. Once we become attached (as in "nailed down") to a person, thing, or thought that attracts us to the point that most of our decisions are driven by it, we are hooked. The same holds true for that which repels us beyond all reason. And almost anything will serve as an object of obsession.

A friend of mine became addicted to road rage, for example, and nearly got arrested for freeway violence before he made the problem the central focus of his prayer life. Another friend is clearly addicted to beauty—she cannot stop herself from buying a lovely painting, whether or not she has the money, and her obsession with art is driving her toward bankruptcy. We can just as easily become attached to our wounds. When we begin to center our thinking around them or rearrange our life in an attempt to avoid the unrelenting pain they generate, as with my raw and aching guilt, we have become imprisoned by them. What does this mean, in practical terms?

First, we find ourselves spending more and more time dwelling on the source of our pain or on the pain itself. It becomes the reference point for the rest of our life, the fulcrum around which everything else must turn. We need to spend increasing amounts of time and energy on the issue or we feel strangely bereft. Second, when we do try to stop thinking about it, we get agitated and nervous, as though undergoing some form of withdrawal. We cannot imagine what things would be like inside us without this central feature in place. Fearfully, we go back to clinging to what we know best. Third, we can no longer count on our willpower to get us out of the trap. Our will is divided against itself, one part determined to remain attached and the other struggling to let go. And finally, our attention becomes distorted; we are so focused on the wound that all our energy goes there. We can't truly love other people when we're addicted to our pain, because we have nothing left over for other concerns.

As May points out, however, the great blessing hidden within addictions—even the deadliest, like alcohol and drugs—is that they reveal our weakness and dependence and put the lie to prideful self-sufficiency. When St. Paul begs the Lord to remove the thorn in his flesh that stubbornly refuses to yield no matter how hard he struggles against it, Jesus responds, "My grace is sufficient for you, for power is made perfect in weakness" (2 Cor. 12:9). We cannot cure ourselves, and when we try, we're like a fly in a spider's web: our increasingly frantic efforts to free ourselves through our own willpower simply bind us faster and tighter. After years of working with seriously addicted clients, May is convinced that our *only* escape from the enslavement of obsessive attachment to a thing, a person, or an idea is through grace.

freedom through grace

St. Paul reminds us that although "all have sinned and are deprived of the glory of God," we are "justified freely by his grace through the redemption in Christ Jesus, whom God set forth as an expiation, through faith, by his blood" (Rom. 3:23–25). Any attempt to set aside an obsessive attachment to guilt must begin with this basic principle: God has *already* freed us from our enslavement to sin through the atoning death of Jesus Christ. Though we will continue to struggle with temptations of the flesh and spirit (Aquinas called this natural weakness in us "concupiscence") and thus will continue to need forgiveness, once we've been baptized, the past is forgiven and we've been freed from the absolute tyranny of sin.

More, even if we go on to fall multiple times during the course of our lives, we *always* have recourse to God's loving mercy. Though we may forever weep tears of healthy compunction for the hurts we have caused, we have no business becoming obsessed with our guilt and allowing it to draw off the energy that could be poured into God's work in the world. Instead of fretting over sins that have already been forgiven, we should be dealing with the very real temptations of the present. Though these, too, can be discouraging, especially when they raise the ghostly specters of the past, Jesus assures us that "whoever endures till the end will be saved" (Mt. 10:22). Obsessive guilt, like all addictions, is life-killing; in contrast, the grace that comes to us through God's forgiveness is death destroying.

However, in order to accept that we've been forgiven and will continue to be as long as we are sincerely repentant, we must really believe that God does not want us to wallow endlessly in old guilt. The opposite holds true: Jesus came to heal us of our guilty wounds in order to free us up for communion with him and for participation in the divine life. When he took our sins upon his shoulders and willingly went to his death on our behalf, he was not only paying our debt to divine justice, he was curing us of our sin-caused wounds. As St. Paul tells us, "Whoever is in Christ is a new creation: the old things have passed away; behold new things have come. And all this is from God, who has reconciled us to himself through Christ and given us the ministry of reconciliation" (2 Cor. 5:17–18).

Today we are so far removed from the system of blood sacrifice that dominated Middle Eastern culture at the time of Jesus' life and death that it is difficult to comprehend (or accept) the logic of the atoning crucifixion. To us, it can easily seem barbaric; if *this* is what God required in order to remit our sins, we think, then how could he possibly be the merciful, loving Abba that Jesus keeps describing? Besides, it's very difficult for us to fathom the notion of collective sin at all anymore. We feel plenty of personal guilt, but the notion of *communal* sin that needs to be expiated is by now nearly extinct. Reading about the Hebrew culture into which Jesus was born—a community that was in many ways far more just, equitable, and concerned with human dignity than the child-sacrificing societies that surrounded it—can help put the atoning crucifixion into context.

The book of Leviticus describes the Mosaic ritual for cleansing the Hebrew community of its accumulated transgressions. Once a year, on the Day of Atonement, two goats were brought to the priests. One was sacrificed and burned. The other was taken to the edge of camp, where the sins of the people were transferred to the head of this "scapegoat," who carried them out into the wilderness inhabited by Satan. Jesus, whom John the Baptist calls "the Lamb of God who takes away the sin of the world," is both the once-and-for-all scapegoat who shoulders the burden of our wrongdoing and also the sacrificial being who sets us free forever from the oppressive guilt that must otherwise be ritually, continually, removed.

Not only did Jesus fulfill the role of a final scapegoat for the entire human race, he also served as its great physician. Throughout the Gospels, he restores sight to the blind, hearing to the deaf, movement to the paralyzed, and reason to the insane or demon-possessed. His message is resoundingly clear: in order to enter the kingdom of heaven, we must first be healed of whatever holds us back. Interestingly, he often tells the people he cures that their sins are being forgiven at the same time. He says this to the paralytic who has been lowered by his friends through the ceiling, and when he is accused of blaspheming, he asks the assembled crowd, "Which is easier to say to the paralytic, 'Your sins are forgiven,' or to say, 'Rise, pick up your mat and walk'?" (Mk. 2:9). According to Jesus, our sinning and our woundedness are different facets of the same basic problem.

What is this problem? Our sin-caused wounds prevent "at-one-ment" with God (the word *atonement* originally meant "to make 'at one'"). Christ has come to rescue a people who are crippled by their sins, whose attention and energy is taken up by their physical ailments or psychic wounds, whose focus is on pain, suffering, and guilt rather than on the joy of communion with God. In this situation, to heal and to forgive is to liberate. And throughout the Gospels, Jesus indeed links these two actions—healing and forgiving—with freedom.

When, for example, he cures a woman who for eighteen years has been unable to stand erect, he tells her, "Woman, you are set *free* from your infirmity" (Lk. 13:12). In the synagogue at Nazareth, he reads out loud from the scroll of Isaiah: "The Spirit of the Lord is upon me, because he has anointed me to bring glad tidings to the poor. He has sent me to proclaim *liberty* to captives, recovery of sight to the blind, to let the oppressed go *free*" (Lk. 4:18). When we allow ourselves to believe we have been forgiven by God and can be forgiven by him again and again, if necessary, we are both healed of our obsessive guilty wounds and set free to take up a new life.

the joy of being forgiven and healed

At the heart of our inability to claim God's liberating forgiveness for ourselves often lies one
of two mistaken notions about the extent of our
own capabilities. The first—very American in
flavor—is that we chart our own course, create
our own lives, and thus, are entirely responsible
for what happens to us. The second, opposite,
misperception is that we are so shaped by
unconscious urges, environmental influences,
and neurological hardwiring that we have very
little control over our destinies. To compound
matters, we rarely think in terms of temptation
anymore, and when we do, we feel as though
we should either be able to defeat it through
our own willpower or, conversely, that we are
fated to succumb because of psychological
predestination.

Jesus comes to offer us a third view of ourselves
and our prospects. According to him, we are
neither entirely self-sufficient nor entirely determined creatures, but instead are an aggravating
mixture of strengths and weaknesses. Even in

the midst of the worst addictions, for example, we retain enough of our own wills to seek help and to make certain decisions—which means we never entirely lose our human freedom. But our tendency is either to exaggerate our level of personal power or to dramatize our supposed helplessness. Jesus tells us that he will provide the grace we need to cope with the reality of our condition: we are in dire need of changing, but we cannot change without help.

Rumer Goden's novel *In This House of Brede* tells the story of Dame Philippa, a highly successful, middle-aged businesswoman who (inexplicably to everyone who knows her) decides to become a nun in a cloistered monastery. Though it is difficult enough to adjust to monastic life after years of independent living, her real challenge in terms of community living is that she now has day-to-day witnesses to her secret pain, an affliction she has always before been able to mask beneath her hard-driving persona. She is immediately recognized by her superiors as a person of great talent, a sincere lover of God, a potentially great blessing to the convent, if it were not for the mysterious shadow of grief or guilt that follows her everywhere.

At a critical point in the story, Philippa is called before her superiors and told that it is time to reveal her secret, that she is being held back in her spiritual life by her refusal to be healed of whatever is so deeply troubling her. And so she finally tells them about the tragic death of her son years before, a loss that she blames on both herself and the nurse that was hired to care for her child. Because she cannot forgive either the nurse or herself, she is imprisoned in her grief and guilt.

Her decision to share the burden with people who love her and can pray for her healing leads to her realization that she *wants* to forgive and be forgiven, she *wants* to let go of the past and move on. When she finally does, she is in every sense set free to live up to her potential within the community and before God. Where before, her trustworthiness was always in question— would she be able to withstand the rigors of monastic life? would she be drawn back into the world?—after her liberation from obsessive guilt and anger, she becomes a healer herself, and eventually the abbess of a new foundation.

Being forgiven means being healed. Both mean liberation.

In emotional terms, we are no longer saddled by the heavy weight of dark memories, urges to go back and rewrite the past, or the temptation toward self-deceptive lying. We can stop living in the old tragedies we have played a part in creating. The result is that we feel a new lightness in our bones, as though we've shed a literal burden. We feel lovable and able to love. Our creative energy is released, and we are suddenly brave enough to trust in it. St. Paul says, "For freedom Christ set us free" (Gal. 5:1), and Jesus tells us that he has come so we "might have life and have it more abundantly" (Jn. 10:10). Finally, through being forgiven, we're able to step into this promised kingdom.

In the sphere of intellect, we understand much more than we ever could when our perspective was so skewed by unforgiven guilt. No longer mired in the murky recesses of the wounded self, we can finally grasp and believe in Christ's message of hope and freedom. The beauty and liberating power of the atonement begins to make sense, and we are filled with gratitude and love for our Messiah. St. Paul urges us to "Rejoice in the Lord always. I shall say it again: rejoice!" (Phil. 4:4), and according to Mark McIntosh's study of Christian epistemology, *Discernment and Truth,* it is this basic, joyful, loving attitude toward life and God that actually provides the ground of knowing.

In the spiritual realm, being freed up and healed by God's forgiveness overcomes our fear of changing. It makes us eager to undergo metamorphosis, to be transformed by grace, to begin the difficult practice of the virtues. More, we can finally pray without getting sidetracked into outworn imagery; we can listen for God's voice without being distracted by the clamoring accusations of cranky old ghosts. In addition, finding our true vocation now becomes a distinct possibility. As Dame Philippa did, we can at last relinquish the belief that if we try to do something for God, we're bound to be ambushed by our own worst self. Most of all, we can give up our misguided quest to control everything that happens to us and rest, instead, in the humility that comes from accepting our dependence on God.

With this growth in spiritual strength and knowledge, we find that our perception of the world has changed. Our vision is being transfigured, and we can now look around us and see that countless others are still being held prisoners to their unresolved guilt and shame. Our hearts are moved with compassion, and, very naturally, as Jesus did among the crowds, we move toward those who are suffering with hands outstretched in healing love. Healed, forgiven, transformed, we become real temples of the Holy Spirit, capable of handling the divine power that Jesus bequeathed to his disciples. Finally, we step into the roles that have always been intended for us: the roles of adopted sons and daughters of God.

trusting in God's love

My many years of obsessing over the possible damage I'd done to my kids took their toll on all of us. I struggled with anxiety, impatience, and dark, lonely nights of self-recrimination that helped set the tone in our home. The bitter internal struggle spilled over onto my stepdaughters too. They symbolized guilt for me—children I'd harmed through my selfish waywardness. And it's hard to warmly, genuinely love people you feel guilty about.

Even after I returned to the church as a new Catholic, I couldn't imagine how to get rid of my burden. Though I dutifully made my first confession, it was tentative and skimpy; I was afraid to say what was really on my mind, or to reveal out loud my fear that God could never *truly* forgive me for what I had done. Besides, as a onetime Lutheran, the very thought of confessing *out loud* to a priest was still a mildly horrifying one. Better to take it slow, I thought, and give God a chance to get used to me and me a chance to get used to this weird business of formally laying bare the heart (or, as my Midwestern relatives would no doubt put it, "airing my dirty laundry in public").

Nearly a year after becoming Catholic—a year during which I'd managed to skate free of every opportunity to expand on my pathetic, minimalist, first-time confession—I happened to be at the hermitage walking with an old friend, a French Canadian monk called Father Bernard, when the subject came up. The moment I began to hem and haw, he was on to me, and though he gave me a few more minutes of casual conversation before he pounced, I knew what was coming next. I was finally going to be making that long overdue, thorough confession. And I was going to be making it to him, a *friend,* a person I frankly preferred to be spared the sordid details of my personal history. I told him that.

He laughed and squinted up at me from under his black beret. "What do you think—that I am going to be shocked?"

"Well—no," I admitted. "Not really. I'm sure you've heard this kind of stuff before. It's just. . . ."

"Look around," he said, gesturing with an open palm toward the sea, the sky and its sprinkling of white stars, the long trail ahead of us, winding down the mountain through copses of redwood and sycamore. "What better setting could you have? We have two hours to make our hike—you can take it as slowly as you want."

What could I say? The night was lovely, the company good, and I'd just run out of my last excuse. "Okaaay," I told him. "But just remember—you asked for it."

Two hours later, as we picked our way across the dark parking lot in front of the bookstore, he stumbled a little and I had to catch his arm. I could tell, by his wavering gait, that he was feeling his age. In fact, he'd gone stone silent for at least the last half hour and seemed to be concentrating on his breathing rather than my story. But I wasn't quite done. I'd started with my earliest memory, after all—being two and throwing an enormous dictionary at infant baby Gail, nursing in my mother's arms—and a couple of hours was hardly enough time to cover the forty years of meanness, jealousy, spite, sexual misconduct, lying, egoistic ambition, and motherly failure in between.

When we got to the door of the chapel, he shuffled to a stop, cast me a pleading look, and said, "Could we go in there now and finish up?"

"It's okay if I'm not quite done?"

"It's okay," he said hastily. "We can save some for next time."

So we went inside the dark church and made our way to the confessional where he took off his beret and draped a stole over his jacket. Then we sat down, knee to knee in two facing wooden chairs, and went through the sacrament of Penance together. At the end, he readjusted his glasses, cleared his throat, and raised one hand in the air for the formula of absolution:

God, the Father of mercies,
through the death and resurrection of
  his Son
has reconciled the world to himself
and sent the Holy Spirit among us
for the forgiveness of sins;
through the ministry of the Church
may God give you pardon and peace,

and I absolve you from your sins
in the name of the Father, and of the Son,
 and of the Holy Spirit.

Then he gave me a tremulous smile and said,
"Can I please go to bed now?"

Back in my room, I sat in front of the window
and grinned out at the stars for another hour at
least. Finally, those old sad sins were gone, dissolved like salt in water. Though I would never
be free of the faint cloud of sorrow that trailed
behind them, they no longer held the power to
reign over my life. Something new had just been
born.

That word *born* made me think of my two
children, who'd come into the world depending
on me to love them, care for them, and help
them grow into adults. They couldn't do it on
their own—and neither could I. Maybe God
saw me the same way I saw them during all those
years they were struggling toward maturity: as
plucky but dependent, well meaning but inexperienced, willing but weak. Maybe he saw me
the way I saw them—as heartbreakingly fragile,

as woefully subject to misdirection and temptation, as frighteningly, perilously precious.

And maybe he saw me now as I'd finally, through his mercy and forgiveness, learned to see them: proof positive of what can happen, despite all the odds, when love is so mightily at work in the world.

conclusion the unforgiving
world vs. the
kingdom of God

CHRIST'S DIFFICULT TEACHING—that if we want to be forgiven by God, we must ourselves offer and accept forgiveness without exception—makes unmistakable good sense when we try to imagine a world completely devoid of forgiveness. Though our present era is filled with the same kind of hostility, strife, and bloodshed that have plagued humankind for eons past, the horrors of our time pale in comparison to a world without any forgiveness in it at all. We truly cannot imagine life without the possibility of forgiveness and reconciliation, for unrestrained animosity would have brought the human species to a bloody end long ago.

Forgiveness, as difficult and delicate as it may be, is—bottom line—our only hedge against self-destruction. It is not an option but a necessity. And slowly but surely, those who work with people in conflict are beginning to come to this realization themselves. From South Africa's justice and reconciliation project to Rwanda's tribal Gacaca courts to Baha'i efforts in world hotspots like Northern Ireland and Jerusalem, people of faith, sociologists, and political scientists alike are taking a serious look at teaching people how to forgive.

Psychologists, too, are finding that mutual forgiveness may be the single most important key to saving marriages, or at least minimizing postdivorce dysfunction in the family. People who have sincerely forgiven one another can let go of the accumulated hurts of the past and sometimes even learn to "re-see" a person they've been married to for decades. Real love can finally bloom, often for the very first time.

People who work with teenagers in crisis, whether these young people be drug-addicted, anorexic, or self-mutilating, are now taking forgiveness seriously. Forgiveness of parents, siblings, or friends can free up young people hovering on the edge of their adult lives to move forward with self-confidence, courage, and a more realistic picture of the human condition. How many lives may have been saved in the past decade if bitter, alienated young people had been taught to forgive before they armed themselves with automatic weapons and murderous rage, rampaging through high school and college campuses?

Our hope is, ultimately, to be found in one event alone: the redemptive self-sacrifice of Christ, who perfectly understood the evil that we can do to others and ourselves. His ascent to the cross was a pitting of divine love against the forces of darkness. During his long hours of agony, he said very little. The few words he did speak, however, had to do with forgiving: "Father, forgive them, they know not what they do" (Lk. 23:34).

A more eloquent demonstration of the central role forgiveness is meant to play in Christian living would be hard to imagine. These words are, literally, among the very last Jesus left us prior to his physical death. That he uttered them in the midst of unspeakable suffering turns them into a powerful symbol of what is humanly possible in a life infused by grace. Countless martyrs throughout Christian history have since testified to this fact.

Not only did Christ leave us with the hope that we, too, might be transformed into forgiving people characterized by agape, but he also left us with the longing for a someday purified creation, a world in which the lamb can safely lie down with the lion. St. John's astonishing visions of the future are recorded in the book of Revelation:

Then I saw a new heaven and a new earth. The former heaven and the former earth were passed away, and the sea was no more. I also saw the holy city, a new Jerusalem, coming down out of heaven from God, prepared as a bride adorned for her husband. I heard a loud voice from the throne saying, "Behold, God's dwelling is with the human race. He will dwell with them and they will be his people and God himself will always be with them. He will wipe every tear from their eyes, and there shall be no more death or mourning, wailing or pain, [for] the old order has passed away." (Rev. 21:1–4).

For we who still live in an unforgiving world, it is good indeed to know that God has promised to someday "make all things new." (Rev. 21:5)

meanwhile, we live and we forgive

However beautiful St. John's revelation may be, we are stuck in the world as it currently is and also in the life God has given us. We are stuck with sins and wounds and shame and sorrow, and sometimes the temptation is to withdraw from all that—to retreat inside a protective shell. Again Christ has anticipated this temptation and made it clear that we are not to succumb. In the powerful image of the vine and the branches, he informs us that we cannot disconnect from one another without losing our lifeblood. We are meant to be one. We are meant to help heal one another. We are meant to forgive, and if possible, to reconcile.

Why? Because we were created for a purpose. And our purpose on Earth is none other than this: To be the face of Jesus for suffering humanity. To love one another as he loved us. To become, despite all our human failings and despite all Satan's efforts to derail us, the very presence of divine love in the world.

acknowledgments

FOR THE PART they have played in the development of my thinking regarding Christian forgiveness, I would like to thank the following people: the monks of New Camaldoli Hermitage (in particular, Fr. Isaiah Tiechert, Fr. Michael Fish, Fr. Bernard Massicote, and Fr. Robert Hale); the oblates of New Camaldoli (especially Janet Walker, Hunter Lillis, Rita King, Danielle Blanchard, and Margaret Joy Granger); the Red Barn meditation group (particularly Karen Lake-Shampain, Wendy Tiechert, and Melanie Northcraft); influential teachers (especially Ken Walker); fellow writers (in particular Deborah Douglas, Tom Grady, and Vinita Hampton Wright); my editors at Paraclete Press (especially Lil Copan and Jon Sweeney); and my family (particularly Gail

Westberg, Gretchen Steer, Mike Huston, and my children: Andrea, John, Kelly, and Greta).

The scriptural quotations in *Forgiveness* are all taken from the New American Bible. I am also greatly indebted to the Catechism of the Catholic Church, and to the work of Josef Pieper, C.S. Lewis, Dallas Willard, Rick Anthony Furtak, and Simon Chan.

notes

introduction

xv   *To truly believe in God without loving him,* Marko Ivan Rupnik, SJ, *Discernment: Acquiring the Heart of God* (Boston: Pauline Books and Media, 2006), 13–16.

chapter one

7   *in his book*   The Sunflower. Simon Wiesenthal, *The Sunflower: On the Possibilities and Limits of Forgiveness* (New York: Schocken Books, 1998), 3–98.

10   *longtime neighborly relations with the family.* Donald B. Kraybill, et al, *Amish Grace: How Forgiveness Transcended Tragedy* (San Francisco: John Wiley & Sons, 2007), 17–46.

10   *for many people it was also deeply troubling.* Ibid., 53–64.

13   *every perpetrator, no matter how savagely he behaves, is also a human being.*   Charles

Villa-Vicencio, interview by Krista Tippett, *Speaking of Faith*, NPR, March 22, 2007.

13   *The philosopher Simone Weil says that cruelty*   Simone Weil, "The Love of God and Affliction," in *Waiting for God*, tran. Emma Craufurd (New York: Harper and Row, 1951), 117–36.

16   *Since God has allowed us to freely choose*   Alvin C. Plantinga, *God, Freedom, and Evil* (Grand Rapids, MI: Eerdman's, 1974), 26–27.

17   *The philosopher Alvin Plantinga, in his book* God, Freedom, and Evil,   Ibid., 28–34.

chapter two

33   *or the Code of Hammurabi of Babylon (1760 BC).*   "Code of Hammurabi," Wikipedia, http://en.wikipedia.org/wiki/Code_of_ Hammurabi.

34   *Where the Hittite laws of restitution require*   *The Harper Collins Study Bible,*   New Revised Standard Version, notes on Exodus 22:1.

37   *Hektor's aged father comes to plead for mercy.*   Homer, *The Iliad*, trans. Richard Lattimore (Chicago: University of Chicago Press, 1961), 442–55.

37   *"A good man cannot be harmed, either in life or death."*   Plato, "The Apology," in *Five*

Dialogues: Euthyphro, Apology, Crito, Meno, Phaedo, trans. G.M.A. Grube (Indianopolis: Hackett, 1981), 44.

chapter three

58 *"I am a sick man. . . .*   Fyodor Dostoevsky, *Notes From the Underground,* trans. Constance Garnett, in *Literature of the Western World,* comp. Brian Wilkie and James Hurt (Upper Saddle River, NJ: Prentice Hall, 1997), 4:1006–76.

62 *For centuries, Lewis says, this curious,*   C.S. Lewis, *Mere Christianity* (New York: Mac-Millan, 1960), 3–7.

64 *"Evil thenceforth became my good"*   Mary Shelley, *Frankenstein,* in *Literature of the Western World,* 2:798 (italics mine).

65 *Even though we accept the law of nature*   Lewis, *Mere Christianity,* 6–7.

68 *Environmentalist David Bella sheds light*   David A. Bella, "Emergence and Evil," *E:CO* 8, no. 2 (2006): 102–15.

70 *As political philosopher Hannah Arendt notes in her classic* Hannah Arendt, *Eichmann in Jerusalem: A Report on the Banality of Evil*   (New York: Viking Press, 1963).

71 *The Catholic teachings on mortal sin*   Harriet A. Luckman and Linda Kulzer, *Purity of Heart in Early Ascetic and Monastic Literature* (Collegeville, MN: Liturgical Press, 1999).

72 *Thomas Merton's spiritual autobiography,* Thomas Merton, *The Seven Storey Mountain* (San Diego: Harcourt Brace and Company, 1976).

75 *C.S. Lewis says that this huffy sense of affront,* Lewis, *Mere Christianity,* 94.

75 *"are mere fleabites in comparison."*   Ibid.

80 *The Eastern Orthodox Church sings of Christ during Easter Vigil*   Vladimir Lossky, *The Mystical Theology of the Eastern Church* (Crestwood, NY: St. Vladimir's Seminary Press, 2002), 153.

chapter four

86 *To counteract the human tendency*   Martha Nussbaum, *Upheavals of Thought: The Intelligence of Emotions* (Cambridge: Cambridge University Press, 2001), 38.

chapter five

105 *However, as Jesuit Marko Rupnik notes in his book*   Rupnik, *Discernment,* 25–27.

118 *When, years later, the truth was finally revealed,*
Douglas Burton-Christie, *The Word in the Desert: Scripture and the Quest for Holiness in Early Monasticism* (New York: Oxford University Press, 1993), 255.

119 *we are still living in "enemy-occupied territory."*
Lewis, *Mere Christianity,* 36.

120 *Evagrius Ponticus speaks about this method*
Evagrius Ponticus, *The Praktikos & Chapters on Prayer,* Cistercian Studies Series 4, trans. John Eudes Bamberger, OCSO (Kalamazoo, MI: Cistercian Publications, 1981).

124 *Modern writers, such as the French monk André Louf,* André Louf, *Teach Us to Pray,* trans. Hubert Hoskins (Cambridge: Cowley Publications, 1992), 7.

125 *Yet no matter what we're able to unearth*
Walter C. Langer, *The Mind of Adolph Hitler: The Secret Wartime Report* (New York: Basic Books, 1972).

126 *As writer Nicholas Delbanco points out*
Nicholas Delbanco, *The Death of Satan: How Americans Have Lost the Sense of Evil* (New York: Farrar, Strauss, Giroux, 1995).

129 *We hear the implicit message of forgiveness*
Mother Teresa, *Come Be My Light: The Private Writings of the "Saint of Calcutta,"* ed.

Brian Kolodiejchuk, MC (New York: Double-day, 2007).

chapter six

142 *The Christian moral life, he believed,*　Soren Kierkegaard, *Training in Christianity* (New York: Vintage, 2004).

142 *the severing of an emotional response*　Rick Anthony Furtak, *Wisdom in Love: Kierkegaard and the Ancient Quest for Emotional Integrity* (Notre Dame, IN: University of Notre Dame Press, 2005), 52–64.

143 *As aesthetes, we want "to have the effect without the cause."*　Ibid, 53.

144 *More admirable by far,*　Ibid, 65–77.

chapter seven

159 *The psychiatrist Barry Grosskopf writes movingly*　Barry Grosskopf, *Forgive Your Parents, Heal Yourself: How Understanding Your Painful Family Legacy Can Transform Your Life* (New York: Free Press, 1999), 55–81, 93–135.

chapter eight

177 *"not attempting to restrain the tears that stream down his cheeks."*　Leo Tolstoy, *Anna Karenin,*

trans. Rosemary Edmonds (Baltimore: Penguin Books, 1964), 13, 438, 439.

chapter nine

203 *Our theological disputes become the point of our Christian identity;* Mark A. McIntosh, *Discernment and Truth: The Spirituality and Theology of Knowledge.* (New York: Crossroad, 2004), 133.

224 *"And in the future life a Christian* St. Symeon the New Theologian, *Magnificat* Vol. 9:12, Jan. 2008, from *The First Created Man, Seven Homilies,* trans. Father Seraphim Rose (Alaska: St. Herman Press, 2001).

chapter ten

246 *We have spurned a gift, crushed a flower,* Matthew and Dennis Linn, *Healing Life's Hurts: Healing Memories Through the Five Stages of Forgiveness* (Mahwah, NJ: Paulist Press, 1993).

chapter eleven

259 *Psychiatrist and spiritual director Gerald May* Gerald May, *Addiction and Grace: Love and Spirituality in the Healing of Addictions* (San Francisco: HarperSanFrancisco, 1998), 1–20.

269 *Rumer Goden's novel* Rumer Goden, *In This House of Brede* (Chicago: Loyola Press, 2005).

272 *according to Mark McIntosh's study* McIntosh, *Discernment and Truth,* 12.

277 *God, the Father of mercies, Catechism of the Catholic Church* (Ligouri, MO: Ligouri Publications, 1994), 1449.

About Paraclete Press

Who We Are

Paraclete Press is a publisher of books, recordings, and DVDs on Christian spirituality. Our publishing represents a full expression of Christian belief and practice—from Catholic to Evangelical, from Protestant to Orthodox.

We are the publishing arm of the Community of Jesus, an ecumenical monastic community in the Benedictine tradition. As such, we are uniquely positioned in the marketplace without connection to a large corporation and with informal relationships to many branches and denominations of faith.

What We Are Doing

Books

Paraclete publishes books that show the richness and depth of what it means to be Christian. Although Benedictine spirituality is at the heart of all that we do, we publish books that reflect the Christian experience across many cultures, time periods, and houses of worship. We publish books that nourish the vibrant life of the church and its people—books about spiritual practice, formation, history, ideas, and customs.

We have several different series, including the best-selling Living Library, Paraclete Essentials, and Paraclete Giants series of classic texts in contemporary English; A Voice from the Monastery—men and women monastics writing about living a spiritual life today; award-winning literary faith fiction and poetry; and the Active Prayer Series that brings creativity and liveliness to any life of prayer.

Recordings

From Gregorian chant to contemporary American choral works, our music recordings celebrate sacred choral music through the centuries. Paraclete distributes the recordings of the internationally acclaimed choir Gloriæ Dei Cantores, praised for their "rapt and fathomless spiritual intensity" by *American Record Guide*, and the Gloriæ Dei Cantores Schola, which specializes in the study and performance of Gregorian chant. Paraclete is also the exclusive North American distributor of the recordings of the Monastic Choir of St. Peter's Abbey in Solesmes, France, long considered to be a leading authority on Gregorian chant.

DVDs

Our DVDs offer spiritual help, healing and biblical guidance for life issues: grief and loss, marriage, forgiveness, anger management, facing death, and spiritual formation.

Learn more about us at our Web site:
www.paracletepress.com, or call us toll-free at 1-800-451-5006.

You may also be interested in...

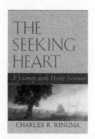

The Seeking Heart
Charles R. Ringma

ISBN: 978-1-55725-446-7
$16.95, Paperback

With Henri Nouwen as your guide, *The Seeking Heart* invites you to the very core of the Christian tradition, where solitude, meditation, prayer, faith, and hope are essential for discerning God's will and finding renewal.

A Little Daily Wisdom
Carmen Acevedo Butcher
Foreword by Phyllis Tickle

ISBN: 978-1-55725-586-0
$14.95, Deluxe Paperback

"Remember kind actions—more than anything else—cause the soul to shine with brilliance."
—Gertrude the Great

Discover the strength, wisdom, and joyful faith of Christianity's legendary women—the medieval mystics. Their honesty and deep love for God will encourage and empower you every day of the year.